FRENCH MODERNIST LIBRARY

Series Editors:

Mary Ann Caws

Richard Howard

Patricia Terry

**Modernities and Other Writings**

# MODERNITIES and Other Writings

# By Blaise CENDRARS

Edited & introduced by
Monique Chefdor
Translated by Esther Allen
in collaboration
with Monique Chefdor

UNIVERSITY OF NEBRASKA PRESS: LINCOLN & LONDON

Library of Congress Cataloging in Publication Data
Cendrars, Blaise, 1887-1961.
[Prose works. English. Selections]
Modernities and other writings / by Blaise Cendrars;
edited and introduced by Monique Chefdor; translated
by Esther Allen in collaboration with Monique Chefdor.
p. cm. – (French modernist library). Includes bibliographical references. ISBN 0-8032-1439-1 (alkaline paper)
1. Cendrars, Blaise, 1887-1961 – Translations into
English. 1. Chefdor, Monique. 11. Title. 111. Series.
PQ2605.E55A225 1992 844'.912–dc20 91-43824 CIP

Typeset in Adobe Garamond and Linotype Futura Bold
Condensed by Keystone Typesetting Co. Printed by
Edwards Brothers, Inc. Designed by Richard Eckersley.

Frontispiece: Blaise Cendrars, circa 1948. Photograph
taken by "Apocalypse," unknown photographer from
Cavaillon, France. Courtesy of the Monique Chefdor
Collection. Gift of Yvonne Leenhardt. Rights reserved.

# Contents

## Acknowledgments

I wish to express my gratitude to the following persons for their assistance in my research on material pertaining to this volume:

Jean Carlo Flückiger, Director of the Blaise Cendrars Studies Center of the University of Bern, Marius Michaud, Curator of the Blaise Cendrars Collection at the Swiss National Library in Bern, and Miriam Cendrars for allowing me to consult the documents of the 'Fonds Cendrars.'

Madame Camus, Research Special Collection Librarian at the Bibliothèque Nationale in Paris for granting me access to the Cendrars/Delaunay letters.

Monsieur Chapon, Curator of the Bibliothèque Doucet, for letting me consult the dossier of 'The Eubage' and Cendrars's letters to Jacques Doucet.

Madame Jacques Henry Levesque for her constant support and the access she gave me to first editions and countless pieces of information.

Scripps College for its support of my research on Cendrars through summer and sabbatical leave grants.

MONIQUE CHEFDOR

## Introduction

Acclaimed by John Dos Passos in 1926 as the 'Homer of the Trans-siberian,' and by Henry Miller in 1938 as 'the most contemporary of contemporaries,' Blaise Cendrars was recognized by his fellow writers and artists long before scholars identified him as a major figure of the twentieth-century avant-garde.[1] As Dos Passos emphasized in his introduction to *Panama,* Cendrars's writings are part of the explosion in the arts which 'had an influence in its sphere comparable with that of the October Revolution in social organization and politics and the Einstein formula in physics.'[2]

Historically, Cendrars belongs to the pantheon of modernists born in the 1880s, which includes the leading figures of twentieth-century letters and art. Guillaume Apollinaire, Andreï Biely, Alexander Blok, Franc Marc, and Robert Musil were all born in 1880; Fernand Léger and Pablo Picasso in 1881; Umberto Boccioni, James Joyce, Igor Stravinsky, and Virginia Woolf in 1882; Alban Berg, Robert Delaunay, and Ezra Pound in 1885; Marc Chagall, Marcel Duchamp, Le Corbusier, Georg Trakl, and Cendrars himself in 1887; T. S. Eliot in 1888; and Jean Cocteau and Abel Gance in 1889. Aesthetically Cendrars in less easily classifiable. He is at once on a par with his contemporaries and far ahead of them, anticipating the present postmodern moment.

Born Frédéric Sauser in 1887 in the Swiss village of La Chaux de Fonds (which also happens to be Le Corbusier's birthplace), Blaise Cendrars spent a peripatetic childhood in various places in Europe, including Naples and Basel, and even in Egypt, while his father pursued a number of unsuccessful business ventures. Cendrars made his striking literary debut in November 1912, when, a few months after arriving in Paris from New York, he published a poem entitled *Les Pâques* (*Easter*), which Jules Romains declared to have determined Apollinaire's 'change of front.' Apollinaire was indeed correcting the proofs of *Alcools* when the Editions des Hommes Nouveaux published *Les Pâques* in November with a leather cover designed by Sonia Delaunay Terk, the Russian-born painter who, with her husband, the Parisian painter Robert Delaunay, would collaborate extensively with Cendrars in the following years. Reprinted in *Du monde entier* (a collection of Cendrars's poetry published in 1919) under the new title 'Les Pâques à New York' (Easter in New York), Cendrars's free-verse confessional poem narrates the physical and spiritual solitude of the poet in the modern Christless city. Its similarities to 'Zone' (the first poem in *Alcools* but the last of that collection's poems to have been written) are as apparent as the two works' differences from each other, and the debate on the priority of Apollinaire versus Cendrars in the breakthrough of twentieth-century French poetry has long divided scholars.[3] Even if those similarities are diplomatically ascribed to the coincidence of two parallel minds, it is clear that Cendrars – exhilarated by his direct experience of the 'universal lyricism' in Berlin, New York, and Moscow, the 'prodigious centers of industrial activity' – brought a breeze of authentic *esprit nouveau* into the postsymbolist and postimpressionist literary circles of Paris.[4]

As he puts it himself in 'The Eiffel Tower': 'In the years 1910 and 1911, Robert Delaunay and I were perhaps the only people in Paris who were talking about machines and art and who were vaguely conscious of the great transformations of the modern world.' There is no evidence that Cendrars knew the Delaunays before his return from New York in 1912. The views of all three on the 'transformation of the modern world' were deeply shared, however, and the collaboration between Cendrars and Sonia gave birth, in 1913, to an undeniable landmark in modernist aesthetics: *La Prose du Trans-sibérien*, a work of art written by Cendrars and illustrated in the 'simultaneous colors' of Sonia Delaunay Terk.

Announced in an advance-order publicity brochure (also illustrated by Sonia Delaunay Terk) as the 'First Simultaneous Book,' the poem was published on a single sheet of paper, two meters long, folded into twelve panels. Cendrars liked to claim that the poem's first printing of one hundred copies would, when unfolded, reach the height of the Eiffel Tower. This unique publication was printed and colored to order at Cendrars's own aptly named Editions des Hommes Nouveaux, which consisted of a secondhand press in an attic at 4 rue de Savoie in Paris.[5] It is doubtful that a hundred copies were ever actually produced, but whatever the number of copies the two artists succeeded in selling, the impact of their creation was immediate and powerful. The advance-order form alone triggered off bitter and picaresque polemics over the claim for priority in the use of the term 'Simultané,' and the so-called 'Querelle du Simultanéisme' was silenced only by the advent of World War I.[6]

*The Prose of the Transsiberian* stands out among all twentieth-century poetic experiments as the work that best captures the prismatic reality of the modern world in its multiplicity – the aesthetic goal that was pursued by the majority of the countless avant-garde movements that flourished throughout Europe in 1913.[7] The poem is also significant as the cornerstone on which Cendrars founded his legendary life story. In a society whose imagination fed on notions of exoticism, dreams of Transatlantic crossings and transcontinental train rides in the style of Valery Larbaud's cosmopolitan dandy Barnabooth, Cendrars was the embodiment of the world-roaming poet, tearing through Paris with the dust of his distant ramblings still on his heels. Whether or not he ever actually boarded the Transsiberian train matters little. What matters, as he once curtly replied to a journalist, is that he made us all take it.

In a short piece of autobiographical writing, *Vol à voiles* (1930),

Cendrars narrates how he jumped out of the third-floor window of his family home in Neuchâtel, Switzerland, to board the first passing train, which sent him to Berlin, Moscow, and Siberia. The discovery of a bona fide passport, issued to the young Freddy when his father took him to Saint Petersburg and arranged a job for him in a Swiss jeweler's shop there, amply demonstrates the mythopoetic nature of the story. The fact remains, however, that at the age of seventeen, the future Cendrars went to Russia and lived there for three years (1904–1907), then went back to Saint Petersburg in 1911 after various comings and goings to Paris, Berlin, Leipzig, and Warsaw, including a brief period in Bern, where he enrolled at the university.[8] He may never have boarded the Transsiberian train, but he certainly saw it in Moscow, which was enough to trigger off the poet's imagination.

While in Saint Petersburg, the future Cendrars had also inevitably lived through the historical 'bloody month' of October 1905 and heard the first rumblings of the Russian revolution. If he was only an observer of history in the making during his Russian experience, he was soon to become an active part of it when he joined the Second Regiment of the Foreign Legion in 1914 in order to defend his adopted country, France. With the Italian singer Canudo, Cendrars was among the first to sign the foreign artists' call to the defense of France. A year later in September 1915 he was to lose his right arm in the battle of the Ferme Navarin in the Marne valley. This amputation haunted him throughout his life but did not limit his world roaming or his prolific subsequent writing. He certainly did not go to New York every weekend, as he once boasted in a radio interview, but as soon as he recovered from his war wound we find him making films in Rome at the Rinascimento studios in 1921, sailing four times to Brazil between 1924 and 1929, inaugurating the *SS Normandy* in 1935, exploring Hollywood in search of the outlaw Al Jennings, whose memoirs *Through the Shadows with O'Henry* he had recently translated, and making frequent trips to Spain and Portugal in the late thirties. In 1940, too old to join the army, he became a war correspondent for the British army. He resigned a year later and withdrew into silence in Aix-en-Provence when the Louvain library was burnt down by the Germans. The writer in him always won over the man of action, but Cendrars's real life never came short of the legend he made of it.

He nonetheless carefully cultivated his legendary image until his death in Paris in January 1961, a few days after he received the Grand Prix Littéraire de la Ville de Paris. When, three years earlier, André Malraux, then minister of culture for the French government, came to Cendrars's home to bestow upon him the title of Commander of the Legion of Honor, the paralyzed poet had not yet revealed his Swiss identity to the public. He was still known as Blaise Cendrars, the 'poet of the entire world,' born at the Hôtel des Etrangers on the rue Saint Jacques in Paris: he actually was what he had chosen to become. The symbolic meaning of the pseudonym he coined for himself during one of his many solitary nights of feverish creation in New York City reveals the young artist's mythopoetic vocation. The combination of embers (Blaise suggests *braise* as well as Saint Blaise) with ashes (*cendres*) and art in Latin (*ars*) or arson in English, leaves no doubt as to the scope of his conception of literary creation as a radical act of renewal and transmutation.

Any attempt to unravel fact from fiction in Cendrars's writings would, then, be a gross misunderstanding of the transmutative power of his work. What is fundamental to the appreciation of the texts presented in this volume is their pivotal position among the avant-gardes in which Cendrars appears at every stage of his writer's life.

Never a literary circle theoretician, Cendrars had direct experience of the new forces that were emerging, before they were incorporated into any movement or trend. By the time he arrived in Paris in 1912 he had already been exposed to the revolutions in art and literature which had burst on other parts of Europe long before they shook the Parisian literary world.

As a result of his Franco-German bilingual upbringing, his readings in the German avant-garde, and his friendships with such figures as Herbert Walden, director of the journal *Der Sturm* in Berlin, and Emil Szittya, the anarchist founder of the review *Die Neue Menschen* in Leipzig, as well as his contact with art groups in Munich, he was familiar with German expressionism long before his French contemporaries had recognized its impact. His early childhood in Naples attuned him to the culture (or the reaction to culture) from which Italian futurism sprang. Later, in Saint Petersburg, he probably came across the poets and artists who were still gathering in the Chien Errant café, and, if he did not have personal contact with the futurist Zaoum movement centered on Khelbnikov, he certainly sensed the first rumblings of Russian futurism. From pre-revolutionary Russia, where he had witnessed the crumbling of the Old World, he went to the New World, to New York City, two years before the Armory Show introduced artists such as Francis Picabia and Marcel Duchamp.

It is not surprising that almost every major avant-garde journal in Europe – *Der Sturm, Die Aktion, Cabaret Voltaire, De Stijl, Valori Plastici, Avanscorpeta, Littérature, Sic, L'Esprit Nouveau, La Caravane, Broom, Montjoie, Les Soirées de Paris* – sought contributions from him. Cendrars shot through the pre-World War I milieu of poetic and artistic experimentation like a laser beam, but he never attached himself to any trend or movement. He was quite aware of being ahead of his time, and states his position very clearly in a letter written to Robert Delaunay in 1917: 'I refuse to contribute to contemporary Parisian journals. They are too corny, too old-fashioned. . . . I don't want to be part of the gang. I am not behind, as you say, but ahead. . . . I have seen a few modern foreign journals. It all belongs to yesterday, not to today. I will be visible tomorrow. Today, I'm working.'[9]

By the mid-1920s he had explored every medium of creative activity. He collaborated on *La Roue* with the filmmaker Abel Gance. He was close to all the major painters of the time (Marc Chagall, Fernand Léger, Georges Braque, Léopold Survage, Amedeo Modigliani, and Chaim Soutine, as well as the two Delaunays), and after Apollinaire's death he began to write art criticism. His ballet *La Création du Monde,* produced in collaboration with Darius Mil-

haud and Fernand Léger, and performed in 1923 by the Ballets Sué-
dois at the Théâtre des Champs Elysées, rivaled any of the productions of the Ballet Russe.

Cendrars worked for a while with Jean Cocteau at the Editions
de la Sirène, where he initiated several collections of innovative
publications. At that time he made another breakthrough as the
author of the best-seller *L'Or* (1925; translated as *Sutter's Gold*, 1936),
which has been translated into thirty-four languages.

After his initial impact as a poet, from then on Cendrars became
better known as a novelist. In 1926 he published *Moravagine* (translated into English in 1970), which was recently adapted for the
screen. *Le Plan de l'Aiguille* (translated as *Antarctic Fugue*, 1948) and
*Les Confessions de Dan Yack* both appeared in 1929, and the latter
almost earned Cendrars a Goncourt Prize.[10] In 1930, he closed the
cycle of these life stories with *Rhum*, a biography of Jean Galmot,
who had served as Guiana's representative in the French National
Assembly. Composed of reportings Cendrars had sent to the Paris
press during the famous trial over Galmot's death, this novel actually questions the very possibility of writing a man's life and strikingly foreshadows the later trend of the so-called nonfiction novel.

In the thirties, Cendrars gave up fiction per se and developed his
own kind of storytelling. In this category we can list *Panorama de la
pègre* (1930), based on reportings on the underworlds of Paris and
Marseilles; *Hollywood, la Mecque du cinéma* (1936), a fanciful report
from Hollywood written for *France Soir; Histoires vraies* (1937), *La
Vie dangereuse* (1938), and *D'oultremer à indigo* (1940), all three 'true
stories' inspired by Cendrars's journeys to Brazil in 1924, 1926, and
1927, and *Chez l'armée anglaise* (1940), war reportings based on his
experience as a war correspondent for the British army in 1939.

In 1941 Cendrars withdrew to Aix-en-Provence. After five years
of silence during World War II, he resumed writing, weaving fiction
and autobiography into a four-volume phantasmagoric chronicle of
his life: *L'Homme foudroyé* (1945; translated as *The Astonished Man*,
1970), *La Main coupée* (1946; translated as *Lice*, 1973), *Bourlinguer*
(1948; translated as *Planus*, 1972), and *Le Lotissement du ciel* (1949).

A monument to the legend of the world-roaming poet-storyteller (the 'Bourlingueur'), these meta- or para-autobiographies form an intricately esoteric mythopoetic construct which has no equal among today's postmodern narratives, and which projects Cendrars's poetic intensity at its highest degree of concentration.[11]

Whether he was working as a poet of the cubist era or as the visionary architect of a postmodern narrative structure, Cendrars's primary concern was always to capture the essence of contemporaneity. Never did he achieve this goal more fully than in the collection of poetic writings presented in this volume. Originally published separately in avant-garde literary journals or as illustrated *livres d'artiste* between 1918 and 1926, they seem, at first, like a loose collection of rather disparate forays into various avant-garde experiments.[12] Neither prose nor poetry, neither essays nor short stories, neither pamphlets nor manifestos, yet to some extent all of these things at once, they strike the reader as modernist texts par excellence, if only for their resistance to classification.[13]

Viewed as a whole, these writings represent Cendrars's work at its highest degree of poetic intensity and they reveal the quintessence of the creative sensibility of this century's first decades. Their unity was emphasized by Cendrars himself, in 1931, when he collected most of them into a volume, published by Grasset, entitled *Aujourd'hui* (Today), a title which underscores Cendrars's vision of his enterprise as the expression of his age. Furthermore, unpublished documents leave no doubt as to the programmatic intent of Cendrars's choice, revealing plans for a much more comprehensive volume to be entitled 'Tout autour d'aujourd'hui' (All around today).[14]

In the end, this ambitious project had to be pared down into the more limited collection published as *Aujourd'hui*. It includes all the texts translated here except *The Eubage* and *The End of the World Filmed by the Angel of Notre Dame*. Internal and external evidence, however, justifies the inclusion of these two texts in the present collection of translations. A list of publication projects, dated February 13, 1917, in one of Cendrars's notebooks, indicates that they are of the same vintage as the contents of *Aujourd'hui*, since they are included in the list.[15] Such a list does not constitute absolute proof that all projects were completed by 1917, but at least it strongly indicates the moment of their conception. Later in his life Cendrars wrote that *The End of the World Filmed by the Angel of Notre Dame* was written during his "most beautiful night of writing," September 1, 1917. As for *The Eubage,* which was sent chapter by chapter to the famous art and manuscript collector Jacques Doucet, Cendrars's letters to Doucet establish that each part of it was composed and sent off in 1917.

*I Have Killed,* also included on the list in Cendrars's notebook, appeared a year later as a small booklet illustrated by Fernand Léger. The two texts announced as 'The Book of Cinema' and 'Preface to the Cinema' became *The ABCs of Cinema,* and the pieces described as 'Poetic Tracts and Art Leaflets' are probably drafts of the articles later published as 'Modernities' in Maurice Magre's magazine *La Rose Rouge.* Only *Profound Today* is omitted from the list. Its first publication, as a small illustrated booklet, is dated 1917, and in all likelihood it had just been completed when Cendrars made the list, since the available manuscript leaves no doubt as to the authenticity of the date that appears on it: February 13, 1917.

Time and again 1917 has been noted as the pivotal year for Cendrars. It is striking that each of these apparently disparate texts, which all epitomize the aesthetics of utmost contemporaneity, was conceived in 1917. In another of Cendrars's letters to Robert Delaunay – a letter which is undated but whose paper, ink, handwriting, and context all indicate the year 1917 – he confesses: 'Everything will happen in its due time and all at once. Like you, I have a store of works that require neither commentaries nor comparisons, so I can wait with confidence. . . . No one knows what I am doing. . . . I don't repudiate my former work, and in the fall I hope to publish *Panama,* which is the old 1830 pre-war stuff again, but which has its impact all the same. I know. . . . None of this matters or will matter when my other works come out.'[16] The other works he refers to are the texts presented in this collection.

Their unity lies far deeper than their chronological concurrence.

The thread which unites them, running from *Profound Today* to *The Eubage,* is one of the fundamental characteristics of the age: the compulsive proclamation of the simultaneous perception of things multiple and diversified through the perpetually whirling gyres of consciousness. The Eubage 'driving on the shores of light,' 'spiraling downward forever,' speeding 'through the human atmosphere like a meteorite,' and 'zigzagging like a question mark' into the final explosion of the space ship of his mind is not very different from the Angel of Notre Dame, with his film in which the 'central fire projects the molecular shadow,' and which runs 'vertiginously backwards' in the final kaleidoscope of images. Both illustrate the contradiction in the 'rosette of consciousness' practiced by the 'spirit scattered everywhere' of *Profound Today.* The poet of *I Have Killed* is essentially the same as the one in *Profound Today,* 'impaled on [his] sensibility.' And the apparent nihilist of *In Praise of the Dangerous Life* who boasts that 'there is no truth, only absurd life waggling its donkey's ears,' and who makes a fetish out of the knives criminals give him, knows also that the secret of the liberation through action he advocates may lie in finding the 'seventh lash from the left eyelid,' as the wise man of India says.

*Profound Today* opens the volume with a declaration of faith in the prodigious exhilaration of the multitudinous as a mode of perception. Described as an 'elegy to Futurism,' it is Cendrars's most effective expression of contemporary reality: a probing into the atomization of consciousness through the experience of unity in today's diversity. It is undoubtedly the best literary counterpart to the theory of simultaneous contrasts, which Cendrars developed in his analysis of Robert Delaunay's paintings. Far beyond the futurists' 'words of freedom,' Cendrars created the true poetics of simultaneity, which capture the age in a more lasting fashion, a simultaneity of the mind and the senses, not merely a simultaneity of the word.

Though the narrative tone of *I Have Killed* and *In Praise of the Dangerous Life* is more personal, they contain a similar manifesto-like expression of today's decentering, multiple reality. In fact these first three texts can be read as a literary triptych, not unlike Survage's triptych *The Fall of Icarus,* which is a visual counterpart to Cendrars's verbal transcription of the modern world.

*The ABCs of Cinema* can serve as a preface to *The End of the World Filmed by the Angel of Notre Dame,* originally written as a screenplay but finally published by Cendrars as a 'novel' when he resigned himself to the fact that his 'film' would not be produced. Cinematographic experiments had inspired many poets during this period – Apollinaire, Max Jacob, Pierre Reverdy, Philippe Soupault, and Louis Aragon, to give a few examples – but Cendrars's work stands out as the most original.[17] *The End of the World* offers an unprecedented model of what could be called 'cinefiction,' and *ABC* is so perceptive in its grasp of the artistic potential of film that it is both a literary work of art and a historical document. It undoubtedly made a strong impression on Abel Gance, whose own work strikingly echoes Cendrars's formulas.[18]

At first glance, *The Eubage* appears to stand alone in Cendrars's oeuvre; its links to the esoteric tradition of the alchemists seem to place it in opposition to the aggressive modernity of the texts that precede it. A closer reading, however, reveals that this cosmogonic journey to the 'hinterland of the sky' is a voyage to the hinterland of the modern mind, where matter is spiritualized and thought materialized in a manner that exceeds the highest anticipation of surrealism. *The Eubage* amplifies and illustrates the visions evoked in the 'integral solitude' and 'anonymous communion' of *Profound Today.* Like Rimbaud's *Illuminations* in the 1880s, it provided an age of the 'dissociation of sensibilities,' as T. S. Eliot would call it, with its testimony to the poetic act of transmutation.

The pieces collectively titled 'Modernities' originally appeared as a series of topical art reviews in the magazine *La Rose Rouge.* They provide a more theoretical exposition of Cendrars's aesthetics. So many poets were writing about art at the time that Francis Picabia satirized them in *Jésus-Christ Rastaquouère:* 'Lyric poets, dramatic poets, you all love art in order to escape from literature, and yet you are nothing but scribblers (*littérateurs*).'[19] Apollinaire's *Art Chronicles* have remained the standard reference for the period. But Reverdy, Jacob, and Soupault, to name only a few, also wrote about their fellow painters. Looking back nostalgically on those days, Cendrars said in an interview: 'Every painter went hand in hand with a poet. Braque with Reverdy, Picasso with Max Jacob; I with Delaunay, Chagall, Léger; Apollinaire with the school of Paris.'[20] Cendrars hints, here, perhaps unwittingly, at a major point of difference between his own writing on art and Apollinaire's: the latter was linked to a 'school,' while Cendrars was personally engaged with individual painters. There is indeed something less official and less comprehensive in Cendrars's comments on his contemporary painters. At the same time he is freer from obligations to the present, and offers uncannily farsighted comments, such as those on the disappearance of schools and movements in favor of individual painters, as well as those on the predominance of color over form. One cannot help thinking of our own art scene since the sixties.

In the context of his other writings, grouped here as they were reprinted by Cendrars himself in *Aujourd'hui,* these essays on art stand as so many theoretical counterparts to the poetic constructs of the other texts. The criticism of the cubist endeavors, the admiration for Picasso, whose work possesses the 'secret cipher of the world,' the understanding of Braque's rigor, and the empathy with Survage's rhythms, building to the discussion of depth and simultaneous perception in Delaunay's work, all serve as an explicit statement of Cendrars's views on the challenge to creativity posed by the 'age of multiplicity,' as Gilles Deleuze called it much later.

Generated by the writer's ambition to probe into the depths of his age, into our profound today, these texts serve as the foundations of Cendrars's creative edifice as well as a major landmark in the entire literary production of the European avant-garde in the first quarter of this century. Cendrars himself thought no less of the achievement these writings represent, as his recently published correspondence with the writer and critic Jacques-Henry Lévesque attests: 'This is the book I would take to a desert island,' Lévesque wrote to Cendrars on January 4, 1939, referring to *Aujourd'hui,* which he had just received in the mail.[21] Cendrars replied: 'Think of this: I reread *Aujourd'hui,* too. There isn't a thing I would take out of it, despite all that has happened. I even have the feeling that no one has ever read it, this book, or else they would talk about literature differently. And about everything!'[22]

May the reader in the last decade of the century echo the writer's confidence in the impact of his writing.

MONIQUE CHEFDOR

## Notes

1. John Dos Passos, 'Homer of the Transsiberian,' *Saturday Review of Literature,* October 16, 1926; repr. in *Orient Express* (New York: Harper, 1927), 155–67. Henry Miller, 'Tribute to Blaise Cendrars,' *T'ien Tsia Monthly* (Shanghai) 7 (1938); repr. in *The Wisdom of the Heart* (New York: New Directions, 1941), 152. Among the major critical studies available in English see the works by Jay Bochner, Mary Ann Caws, Monique Chefdor, and Marjorie Perloff listed in the Bibliography.

2. John Dos Passos, trans., Blaise Cendrars, *Panama* (New York: Harper, 1931).

3. See Monique Chefdor, *Blaise Cendrars,* Twayne World Authors Series, 571 (Boston: G. K. Hall, 1980), 144–45.

4. Blaise Cendrars, *Oeuvres complètes,* vol.6 (Paris: Denoël, 1961), 55–56.

5. Before it became an independent press, Les Hommes Nouveaux was a Franco-German quarterly which Cendrars founded in 1912 with Marius Hanot and Emil Szittya, a German writer from Leipzig; both Szittya and Hanot were vaguely connected with anarchist groups. Only one issue of the promisingly titled journal is known, dated October 1912. It is filled with articles written by Cendrars, Diogène, and Jack Lee, all pseudonyms of Frédéric Sauser.

6. See Monique Chefdor, 'Blaise Cendrars et le Simultanéisme,' *Europe* 566 (June 1976); and Susan Taylor Horrex, 'Blaise Cendrars and the Aesthetics of Simultaneity,' *Dada Surrealism* 6 (1976).

7. See Liliane Brion-Guerry, ed., *L'Année 1913: Les formes esthétiques de l'oeuvre d'art à la veille de la première guerre mondiale* (Paris: Klincksieck, 1977).

8. Biographical data on Cendrars in English can be found in the works

listed under Jay Bochner and Monique Chefdor in the Bibliography. Miriam Cendrars wrote an extensive life of Cendrars, mostly based on Cendrars's own writings; it was published, in French, in 1984 by Balland's, and reprinted in 1987 by Points Seuil. My introduction to *Complete Postcards from the Americas* provides a concise but complete and accurate summary of Cendrars's life. In *Europe* 566 (June 1976), I compiled a chronology of all verifiable biographical data to date. It shows that Cendrars's actual life was just as rich in events as the legendary one. Another brief overview of Cendrars's career in English is my introduction to *Studies in Twentieth Century Literature* 2 (Spring 1979), an issue which Jay Bochner and I edited. A brief chronology of Cendrars's life is also available in the same issue.

9. Undated manuscript letter to Robert Delaunay, Delaunay Special Collection, Bibliothèque Nationale, Paris. The letter's context, paper, ink, and handwriting all indicate the year 1917.

10. Directed by Philippe Pilard, who wrote the screenplay in collaboration with Miriam Cendrars, *Moravagine* was shown in February 1990, in four episodes, on the French television channel Sept and again in March on FR3. It is a French-Hungarian co-production (SFP, FR3 and LA7 [France] and MTV [Hungary]). *The Confessions of Dan Yack* (1929) was so close to being awarded the Goncourt Prize that a few years ago one could still find copies of it marked 'Prix Goncourt, 1929' on sale. According to the newspapers of the day, the prize went to Roland Dorgelès instead of Cendrars because Cendrars refused to provide the jury with proof of his French nationality. Cendrars had become a naturalized French citizen while still in the hospital after losing his right arm in the battle of La Ferme Navarin in September 1915. In 1929, he couldn't be bothered to dig out his naturalization papers for the Goncourt academy and was quoted as saying, 'I gave my right arm to France. Why the hell do they need papers to prove I became a French citizen!'

11. On Cendrars and postmodern narratives see Monique Chefdor, 'Blaise Cendrars outre-atlantique: Perspectives postmodernistes,' in *Blaise Cendrars vingt ans après,* ed. Claude Leroy (Paris: Klincksieck, 1982), 39–47 and 228–31.

12. See Bibliography. Angel Zaragga illustrated *Profond Aujourd'hui;* Jean Hecht, *L'Eubage;* and Fernand Léger, *J'ai tué* as well as *La fin du monde*

*filmée par l'Ange Notre Dame.* These volumes have now become priceless collectors' items.

13. The first in a series of issues of *La Revue des Lettres Modernes* dedicated to critical studies of Cendrars's works actually singles them out as 'unclassifiables': *Blaise Cendrars: Les Inclassables (1917–1926),* ed. Claude Leroy, *La Revue des Lettres Modernes* 782–785 (1986). The directors of the series are Claude Leroy and Monique Chefdor.

14. Tables of contents in manuscript of several versions of the projected book, Blaise Cendrars Collection, National Swiss Library, Bern. They all list the texts collected here along with others that were never published, and perhaps never written.

15. *Inédits Secrets,* ed. Miriam Cendrars (Paris: Club Français du Livre, 1969), 409.

16. Delaunay Special Collection, Bibliothèque Nationale, Paris.

17. See Jean Epstein, *Ecrits sur le Cinéma, 1921–1953,* vol.1 (Paris: Seghers, Cinéma Club, 1974).

18. Cendrars had worked with Abel Gance on *La Roue* in 1920 and later had a contract of his own with the studio Rinascimento in Rome. In spite of his passion for the cinema Cendrars never succeeded in carrying out his plans in this area. The story of Cendrars's relationship with the film arts has been discussed by Philippe Pilard, in 'Cinéma de rêve, rêve de cinéma,' in *Sud,* 1988, 123–33, and by Maurice Mourier, 'Quand Cendrars rêve cinéma,' in *Blaise Cendrars: Les Inclassables,* 87–112. The work by Gance which most closely echoes *The ABCs of Cinema* is an article entitled 'Le temps de l'image est venu,' in *L'art cinématographique,* vol.2 (1927): 83–102. Whatever the extent of Cendrars's association with Gance, the Bern documents I refer to above demonstrate that Cendrars's writings on film arts and his conception of *The End of the World* as a film script preceded his collaboration with Abel Gance. The publication of fragments in 1916 and 1918 give evidence of the early genesis of this script in Cendrars's mind.

19. Francis Picabia, *Jésus-Christ Rastaquouère,* illus. G. Ribbemont Dessaignes (Paris: Collection Dada, 1920), 14.

20. André Parinaud, 'La peinture et ses témoins,' *Arts* 33 (November 16, 1951).

21. Lévesque to Cendrars, January 4, 1939, letter 87, *'J'écris. Écrivez-moi.'* *Correspondance Blaise Cendrars–Jacques Henry Lévesque, 1924–1959,* ed. Monique Chefdor, vol.9 of Blaise Cendrars, *Oeuvres complètes* (Paris: Denoël, 1991), 122.

22. Cendrars to Lévesque, January 27, 1939, letter 92, ibid., 126.

**Modernities and Other Writings**

**Profound Today**

I no longer know if I'm looking with my naked eye at a starry sky or at a drop of water through a microscope. Since the origin of the species, the horse moves, supple and mathematical. Machines are already catching up, moving ahead. Locomotives rear and steamships whinny on the water. Never will a typewriter commit an etymological spelling error, but the man of intellect stammers, chews his words, and breaks his teeth on antique consonants. When I think all my senses burst into flame and I'd like to violate all beings, and when I give rein to my destructive instincts I find the triangle of a metaphysical solution. Inexhaustible coal mines! Cosmogonies find a new life in trademarks. Extravagant signboards over the multicolored city, with the ribbon of trams climbing the avenue, screaming monkeys hanging on to each other's tails, and the incendiary orchids of architectures collapsing on top of them and killing them. In the air, the virgin cry of trolleys![1] The material world is as well trained as an Indian chief's stallion. It obeys the faintest signal. Pressure of a finger. A jet of steam sets the piston going. A copper wire makes the frog's leg jerk. Everything is sensitized. It is all within range of the eye. You can almost touch it. Where is man? The gesturings of protozoa are more tragic than the history of a woman's heart. The lives of plants more stirring than a detective story. The musculature of the back in motion dances a ballet. This piece of fabric should be set to music and that jar of preserves is a poem of ingenuity. The proportion, angle, appearance of everything is changing. Everything moves away, comes closer, cumulates, misses the point, laughs, asserts itself, and gets aggravated. Products from the five corners of the world turn up in the same dish, on the same dress. We feed on the sweat of gold at every meal, every kiss. Everything is artificial and very real.[2] Eyes. Hands. The immense fleece of numbers on which I lay out the bank. The sexual furor of factories. The turning wheel. The hovering wing. The voice traveling along a wire. Your ear in a trumpet. Your sense of direction. Your rhythm. You melt the world into the mold of your skull. Your brain hollows out. Unsuspected depths, in which you pluck the potent flower of explosives. Like a religion, a mysterious pill activates your digestion. You get lost in the labyrinth of stores where you renounce yourself to become everyone. With Mr. Book you smoke the twenty-five-cent Havana featured in the advertisement. You are part of the great anonymous body of a café. I no longer recognize myself in the mirror, alcohol has blurred my features. He espouses the novelty shop as he would the first passerby. Every one of us is the hour sounding on the clock. To control the beast of your impatience you rush into the menagerie of railway stations. They leave. They scatter. Fireworks. In all directions. The capitals of Europe are on the trajectory of their inertia.[3] The terrible blast of a whistle furrows the continent. Overseas countries lie still within the net. Here is Egypt on camelback. Choose Engadine for winter sports. Read Golf's *Hotels* under the palm trees. Think of four hundred windows flashing in the sun. You unfold the horizon of a timetable and dream of southern islands. Romanticism. Flags of countryside float at the windows while flowers fall from the garlands of the train and take root and names, forgotten villages! On the move, kneeling in the accordion of the sky through the telescoped voices. The most blasé go furthest. Motionless. For entire days. Like Socrates. With an activity in the mind. The Eiffel Tower sways on the horizon. The sun, a cloud, anything is enough to stretch it or shrink it. The metal bridges are just as mysterious and sensitive. Watches set themselves. From every direction ocean liners move toward their connections. Then the semaphore signals. A blue eye opens. The red one closes.[4] Soon there is nothing but color. Interpenetration. Disk. Rhythm. Dance. Orange and violet hues devour each other. Checkerboard of the port. Every crate is heaped with what you earned by inventing that game, Dr. Alamede.[5] Steam-driven cranes empty thunder from their hampers. Pell-mell. East. West. South. North. Everything turns cartwheels along the docks while the lion of the sky strangles the cows of twilight. There are shiploads of fruit on the ground and on the rooftops. Barrels of fire. Cinnamon. European women are like subaqueous flowers confronting the stern laboring of longshoremen and the dark red apotheosis of machines. A tram slams into your back.[6] A trap door opens under your feet. There's a tunnel in your eye. You're pulled by the hair to the fifteenth floor. Smoking a pipe, your hands at the faucets – cold water, hot water – you think of the captain's wife, whose knee you will soon surreptitiously caress. The golden denture of her smile, her charming accent. And you let yourself slip down to dinner. The tongues are stuffed. Everyone must grimace to be understood. Gesticulate and laugh loudly. Madame wipes her mouth with her loincloth of a napkin. Boeuf Zephir. Café Euréka. Pimodan or Pamodan. Seated in my rocking chair I'm like a Negro fetish, angular beneath the heraldic electricity. The orchestra plays *Louise*. To amuse myself, I riddle the fat body of an old windbag that is floating at the level of my eyes with pinpricks. A deep-sea diver, submerged in the smoke from my cigar, alone, I listen to the dying music of sentimentality that resonates in my helmet. The lead soles of my boots keep me upright and I move forward, slow, grotesque, stiff-necked, and bend with difficulty over the swamp life of the women. Your eye, sea horse, vibrates, marks a comma, and passes. Between two waters, the sex, bushy, complicated, rare. This cuttlefish discharges its ink cloud at me and I disappear into it like a pilot. I hear the engine of the waters, the steel forge of leeches. A thousand suction pores function, secreting iodine. The skin turns gelatinous, transparent, incandesces like the flesh of an anemone. Nerve centers are polarized. All functions are independent. Eyes reach to touch; backs eat; fingers see. Tufts of grassy arms undulate. Sponges of the depths, brains gently breathe. Thighs remember and move like fins. The storm rips out your tonsils. A scream passes over you like the shadow of an iceberg. It freezes and sunders. The being reassembles itself with difficulty. Hunger draws the limbs together and gathers them around the vacuum of the stomach.[7] The body dons the uniform of weight. The spirit, scattered everywhere, concentrates in the rosette of consciousness. I am man. You are woman. Good-bye. Everyone returns to his room. There are shoes in front of the door. Don't confuse them. Mine are yellow. The valet is waiting for his tip. I give him the shield from my coat of arms. I've forgotten to sleep. My glottis moves. This attempt at suicide is regicide. I'm impaled on my sensibility. The dogs of night come to lick the blood running down my legs. They turn it into light. The silence is such that you can hear the mechanism of the universe straining. A click. Suddenly everything is one notch larger. It is today. A great foaming horse. Diseases rise to the sky like stars on the horizon. And here is Betelgeuse, mistress of the seventh house. Believe me, everything is clear, ordered, simple, and natural. Minerals breathe, vegetables eat, animals emote, man crystallizes. Prodigious today. Probe. Antenna. Door-face-whirlwind. You live. Eccentric. In integral solitude. In anonymous communion. With everything that is root and summit and that throbs, revels, jubilates. Phenomena of this congenital hallucination which is life in all its manifestations and the continual activity of consciousness. The motor spirals. The rhythm speaks.[8] Chemistry. You are.

CANNES, FEBRUARY 13, 1917

# I Have Killed

They're coming from every horizon. Day and night. A thousand trains spew out men and material. Evening. We cross a deserted city. There is a large modern hotel in this city, tall and square: the G.H.Q. Cars with pennants, packing cases, an oriental swinging chair. Distinguished young men in impeccable chauffeur's attire talk and smoke. A yellow novel on the sidewalk, a spittoon, and a bottle of eau de Cologne. Behind the hotel there is a small villa tucked back beneath the trees. You can barely see it. A vague white shape. The road passes in front of the iron gate, turns, and runs along the estate wall. We march onto a sudden thick layer of fresh hay, which absorbs the sluggish noise of the thousands and thousands of oncoming army boots. All you hear is the swish of arms rhythmically swinging, the clink of a bayonet, a watch fob, the dull thud of a canteen. A million men breathing. Voiceless pulsation. Involuntarily, each of us straightens and looks at the house, the general's little house. Light filters through the half-closed shutters, and in that light an amorphous shadow moves back and forth. It's HIM. Have pity on the commander-in-chief's insomnias, he wields the table of logarithms like a prayer machine. A calculation of the probabilities[1] stuns him motionless. Silence. It's raining. At the end of the wall, no more straw. We fall and flounder in the mud again. It's pitch dark. The marching songs ring out with renewed vigor:

*Catherine has pig's feet*
*Ugly ankles*
*Knees that knock*
*A moldy crotch*
*And rotting breasts*

Here are the historic roads leading up to the front.

*Ours are the dames*
     *With hair on their asses*
*We'll see them again*
     *When the troops* (repeat)
*We'll see them again*
     *When the troops come home*
. . . . . . . . . . . . . .

*Soldier, get your gear*
     *Not seen, not taken*
          *My old pals*
*Another Arab gets it in the ass*
     *In the Sarge's bunker*
. . . . . . . . . . . . . .

          *Father Grunt*
     *Pull down your pants*
     *Look! It's a sausage!* (three times)
*For Swiss, Alsatians and Lorrains*
. . . . . . . . . . . . . .

     *Bang! goes the Arbi*
          *The jackals are over there*
. . . . . . . . . . . . . .

*One fine evening in early spring*
     *A troop was marching way far south*
          *Then the battle of Af' breaks out*
*Breaks out and out and out again*
     *Save the Tonkinese*
          *Within three months they're out*
. . . . . . . . . . . . . .

The trucks rumble on. To the left, to the right, everything is moving heavily, weightily. Everything progresses by jolts and jerks in the same direction. Columns and masses rattle along. All vibration. It smells of inflamed horse's ass, tool box, carbolic acid, and aniseed. The air is so heavy, the night so stifling, the fields so fetid that it's like swallowing rubber. Old Pinard's stinking breath poisons nature. Hooray for cheap wine in the belly burning like a scarlet medal! An airplane suddenly takes off in a tattoo of backfire. The clouds swallow it up. The moon rolls along behind. And the poplars lining the national highway spin like the spokes of a vertiginous wheel. The hills pitch downward. The night gives in under the pressure. The veil is torn. Everything cracks, bursts, booms out at once. Everything ablaze. A thousand explosions. Flames, fires, blasts. An avalanche of gunshots. Roaring. Barricades. The steam-hammer. Profiled against the glare of the firing shots: oblique, frantic men, the pointed end of a sign, a mad horse. Flutter of an eyelid. Blink of the magnesium flash. Snapshot. Everything disappears. We saw the phosphorescent sea of trenches and the black holes. We pile into the parallel lines of departure, mad, hollow, haggard, soaked, exhausted, thrashed. Long hours of waiting. Our teeth chatter beneath the shells. Long hours of rain. A chill down the spine. A pinch of tobacco.[2] Finally a goosepimpled dawn. Devastated countryside. Frozen grass. Dead soil. Suffering pebbles. Cruciferous barbed wire. An eternal waiting. We are beneath the vaulted dome of the shells, listening to the big ones coming into the station. There are locomotives in the air, invisible trains, crashes, smash-ups. We count out the double beat of the *rimailhos*.[3] The panting of the 240. The bass drum of the 120 long. The rumbling 155, spinning like a top. The insane meow of the 75. An arch opens over our heads. Sounds drop out of it in couples, male and female. Gnashings. Hisses. Ululations. Brays. It coughs, spits, trumpets, shouts, cries, moans. Steel chimeras and rutting mastodons. Apocalyptic mouth, open sack, from which inarticulate words fall, enormous as drunken whales. It connects, makes sentences, takes on significance, intensifies. It becomes explicit. A peculiar ternary rhythm can be discerned, a particular cadence, like a human accent. Eventually the terrifying noise is no more noticeable than the sound of a fountain. It reminds us of a jet of water, a cosmic jet of water, regular, ordered, continuous, and mathematical. Music of the spheres. Breath of the world. I distinctly see an ample female bosom, gently heaving with emotion. It rises and falls. It's round.[4] Powerful. I think of Baudelaire's poem *The Giantess*. A silver whistle. The colonel leaps forward, arms outstretched. It's H hour. We march to the attack, cigarettes at our lips. Immediate rat-a-tat of the German machine guns. The coffee grinders turn. The bullets sputter. We go forward, raising our left shoulders and twisting our shoulderblades over our faces, every bone in our bodies disarticulated so that we can become our own shields. Our temples burn with fever, anguish is all over us. We are taut. But we march on anyway, calm and in formation. No more ranking officers. Instinctively we follow the one who has always been the most composed, often a lowly private. No more bluff. There are still a few swashbucklers who get themselves killed yelling 'Vive la France!' or 'For my wife!' Usually the one who's most taciturn takes command and leads the way, followed by a few hysterics. This group stimulates the others. The braggart makes himself scarce. The ass brays. The coward hides. The weakling falls to his knees. The thief abandons you. Some of them will even pick your pocket beforehand. The chickenhearted skitter to the trenches. Some play dead. And a whole troop of poor guys get themselves bravely killed without knowing how or why. And they fall! Now the grenades are exploding as if under deep water. We're surrounded by flames and smoke. And a demented fear knocks you into the German trench. After a vague flurry we recognize each other. We organize the newly taken position. The rifles fire themselves. We are there all of a sudden among the dead and wounded. No respite. 'Forward! Forward!' We don't know where the order is coming from. And we leave, abandoning the plunder. Now we're marching through tall grass. We see demolished cannon, exposed mines, fields seeded with shells. Machine guns fire at your back. There are Germans everywhere. We have to cross barrages of gunfire. Huge black Austrians who squash an entire section. Limbs fly through the air. A gob of blood hits me right in the face. We hear lacerating screams.

We jump over abandoned trenches. We see heaps of corpses, vile as bundles of rags; shell-craters brimming like garbage cans; pots filled with nameless things, juices, meats, clothing, excrement. Then, in the corners, behind the bushes, in a sunken path, ridiculous dead men, frozen like mummies, making a little Pompeii. The planes are flying so low you have to duck. Over that way is a village to be taken. A big job. More troops arrive. The bombing starts up again. Winged torpedoes, mortars. Half an hour goes by and we plunge. Twenty-six of us make it to the position. A prestigious decor of collapsing houses and eviscerated barricades. This must be cleaned up. I have the honor of being issued a switchblade. A dozen of them are distributed, along with several large melinite bombs. Here I am, *eustache*[5] in hand. That's what it comes down to, the whole immense war machine. Women working themselves to death in factories. A population of laborers toiling deep in the mines. The striving of scholars and inventors. The whole of human activity has to pay its toll. The wealth of a century of intensive labor. The experience of several civilizations. All over the world people are working for me alone. Ores come from Chile, canned foods from Australia, leather from Africa. America sends us machine tools, China sends us workmanship. The field kitchen's horse was born in the pampas of Argentina. I'm smoking Arabian tobacco. I have Batavian chocolate in my rucksack. Men's hands and women's hands have made everything I wear. All races, all climates, all beliefs have collaborated. The most ancient traditions and the most modern techniques. The entrails of the globe and the standards of good behavior have been radically disrupted; virgin lands have been exploited, inoffensive beings have been schooled in an inexorable trade. Entire countries have been transformed in a single day. Water, air, fire, electricity, radiography, acoustics, ballistics, mathematics, metallurgy, fashion, superstitions, travels, the arts, the lamp, the table, the family, and the history of the universe are the uniform I wear. Liners cross the oceans. Submarines dive. Trains run on. Files of trucks reverberate. Factories explode. In the cities, crowds rush to the movies and fight for the newspapers. Deep in the country, peasants plant and harvest. Souls pray. Surgeons operate. Financiers get richer. Godmothers write letters. A thousand million individuals have consecrated their day's activity, their strength, their talent, their science, their intelligence, their habits, their feelings, their hearts to me. And here I am, today, knife in hand. Bonnot's *eustache.* 'Long live mankind!' I grip a cold truth, summoned from a sharp blade. I am right. My young athletic past will be enough.[6] Here I am, nerves taut, muscles tensed, ready to leap into reality. I've braved torpedoes, cannon, mines, fire, gas, guns, the whole blind, systematic, demoniac, anonymous machinery. I'm going to brave man. My counterpart. An ape. Eye for eye, tooth for tooth. The two of us now. Face to face. And the fist's blows, the knife's thrusts. Merciless. I jump on my antagonist. I slash him terribly. The head is almost detached. I've killed the Hun. I was faster and more alert. More direct. I was the first to strike. I have the sense of reality: me, the poet. I acted. I killed. Like someone who wants to live.

NICE, FEBRUARY 3, 1918

# In Praise of the Dangerous Life

Once more everything changes entirely and starts all over again. 'Give me the seventh lash from the left eyelid, the seventh from the upper row, counting from the tear duct,' said the wise man of India. Contemplation. Cat's-eye. Objective. The iris of his crystalline pupil enlarged, contracted, spun like the cylinder of a Bell-Howell. We're filming! A tall white fig tree untangled like the sun's hair and a thousand branches fell to take root instantly. In this forest of vivid, glistening leaves, hard, round, and sonorous as gramophone disks, the cries of the wild animals were mingled with the nasal voice of man coming down from the flowering antenna of the lianas. Radiotelephony. The king and queen are checkmated if the sky is a checkerboard and the sun freezes cubically. But in solitude, as if in response to the knife-sharpener's call, thought moves, is displaced, leaves the center to strike sparks on the periphery. As the human voice fades and echoes weakly, a little bell lost in the depths of worlds, you discover that you're holding a scalpel. Today, I am at the antipodes. What is it that circles me? An insect, a bird, a rattlesnake? I am stalking game. I hold my breath. I aim. There is an eye at each end of the line of sight. Everything gluts. The shot fires. A howl. An animal's vast groan and a frantic race through the copse of memory. There are traces of blood. A faint gleam in the shadows. It is dying in its lair. Night falls. The moon rolls along the edge of the appalled sea. Bang! An elephant on the ground. A tapir. A bear, a gazelle, a peccary. Your heart. The world. A duck-billed platypus. Take off your helmet. Wipe your forehead. Eat, drink, smoke, camp. Take off your heavy, painful boots. Lie down. Sleep. Your head will quickly be cleansed in the anthill of the sky. What a beautiful trophy: a bleached skull! You'll take it home and hang it over a cradle. It will be made to speak again, with the help of a spring and some tiny, meticulous gears, a funnel concealed in its mouth. 'Give me a fulcrum and I'll lift the world,' the infantile voice of Archimedes was already murmuring. And he could rest no more. I will lift you, but, where will I set you down? On a dissection table or in a useless museum? Lovely label. A serial number. A capital letter. A word ending in -us. A card in a file. Some words written in red ink. If you want to know who I am, consult a dictionary and all the encyclopedias. Don't forget bookmarks and cross-references. Leaf through. Moisten your finger. Don't skip a single page. You'll end up reading all the books in all the great libraries of the nations and you'll end up making your hole in them like a worm through pulp. You'll eat them because no two pages taste alike. This will give you a hearty appetite. You'd like to know. To know. What? The tree of Science, like those of this forest or the fig tree under which the wise old man of India mutters on, doesn't have two identical leaves. You can always search. There is no unity. Equip yourself with magnifying glasses, with microscopes, with chemical reagents, with a film developer, an atlas, a herbarium, I defy you to find two leaves alike, two palms the same. Two blades of grass, two thoughts, two stars. Two synonymous verbs. In any language in the world. There is no absolute. So there is no truth, only absurd life waggling its donkey's ears. Wait for it, watch for it, kill it. Arm yourself well; you'll have to fire again immediately. One bullet behind the ear and the other in the region of the heart. Without a second's hesitation. Because of its trunk, because of its tail. Because of its terrifying belly that crushes you. Because of its carapace, its claws, its teeth, its sting, its fetid odor, its asphyxiating breath, its inflamed anus, its venomous suckers. Because of the hooked wings from which it suspends itself head down to piss like a female vampire on passers-by. The scalp hit by this oily spray goes bald. The brain ferments. Gold tarnishes. Copper rusts. Crystal clouds over. Everything is phosphorescent, covered with verdigris, and ends up exploding like sunspots. Oh! Listen, everyone, listen to the story of the werewolf. I met him one Easter Sunday in the little prison of Tiradentes. He was white. He'd been in prison for eighteen years. He'd worked for a long time on the construction of the Sul-Mineira railway, laying ties and fastening thousands of bolts and rivets. Then he became a foreman, and finally he was made supervisor of work on the bridge over the Rio das Velhas. The day of the railway's inauguration he was named inspector general of Section B, from the 101st kilometer to Divinopolis. He had taken his place in the private car of the great English engineer. He was dressed in a brand new uniform and proudly sported a huge officer's cap trimmed with gold which he was also wearing for the first time that day. As the official train entered the station, he could no longer contain himself. He leapt onto the platform before the train had stopped. His rival was in the crowd. In the first row of onlookers. Right next to the members of the Municipal Council. He hurls himself onto him, his long Pernambucan knife in hand. He slices his rival's carotid arteries. He opens his chest. He tears out his heart. And before the fanfare's measure is finished, while the bass drum is still pounding at full force, he bites into the palpitating heart and swallows it. All round. Bim, boom, and bim, boom, boom. He lets himself be arrested without putting up the least resistance. The front of his shirt is covered with blood and he's lost his new cap in the uproar. When I interrogate him on the motives for his act, already imagining some fabulous theory of atavism – doesn't Captain Cook speak of savages who ate the hearts of their most valiant enemies in order to incorporate their virtues? and doesn't the extraordinary German adventurer Peter Kolb in his book *Caput Bonae Spei Hodierum, Nuremberg, 1719* tell the story of a great black king who used to cut off the virile members of the Hottentot kinglets whose thrones he usurped? and who devoured strings of genitalia in order to become King of Kings, the Conquerer, the Invulnerable in the eyes of his new subjects—one particular day he swallowed 171 members and 213 testicles; the giant tom-toms stood in front of the king's hut, and there was a large crowd; all the people thronged there to take part in the festivities; sorcerers and *griots* were dancing; the revelry continued all night, an orgy of bitter beer; *at dawn the royal belly was sated,* says the old author, *then those present threw themselves upon each other to rip off each other's balls and become chiefs in their turn* – while I'm imagining some fabulous theory of atavism where lust, adventure, and gold mingle with sunstroke, plunder, and rape in the far-off sixteenth century when the Portuguese trooper coupled furiously with Negresses and Indian women to populate the immensity of the Brazilian forest with Mamluk offspring, clearing a patch of land, controlling his fear and becoming the feverish master of bush, animals, savages, and a million superstitions, my man tells me: 'That's not it at all, Monsieur. Don't forget that I'm white. Of Dutch origins, pure Protestant. I've always worked for the railroads, always conscientiously. I've even driven locomotives. I never once strayed from the strict instructions of my superiors and I always obeyed the rules. Not so much from routine but, rather, because life is dangerous today and an accident can happen so quickly. I have a sense of responsibility, I do. See, you have to know how to take the curves without slowing down, how to go over the shaky bridges at top speed to avoid catastrophe, and all the rules in the world can't help you. You have to have initiative. That's what I finally understood. As much automatism as you like, but don't forget your personality and let it be there for you to make use of at the precise second. So, that day, when they had named me inspector general of the railway, Section B, and I was riding in the private car of the great English engineer with my new cap on, and I had every reason to be proud of the confidence of my superiors, my good conduct, my career, when I believed I had arrived, I understood all at once that that train was taking me nowhere. I would have been the laughingstock of the country with my red cap. I jumped from the moving train and hurled myself on my rival, a scrawny upstart, a greenhorn. He had only been here for three months, filling out forms in offices and bothering everyone to make himself look zealous. He'd been named inspector general of Section A to create a spirit of competition between the two of us, as if I needed to be stimulated – me, who worked myself to exhaustion to get the train across the swamplands, who built the tracks on piles on my own initiative.[1] I've always behaved toward the Company like a man. What humiliation!' Outside, the Easter evening procession stopped beneath the prison windows. Several hundred blacks stood in the plaza. They wore shirts and held lighted candles in their hands. The old women and small children wore masks. A group of young cowherds was leading a donkey; tied to its back was a manne-quin stuffed with gunpowder, firecrackers, rockets, and flares. It was an effigy of Judas Iscariot that they were taking out of the city to set on fire and explode. Standing on a carpeted podium, a young hunchbacked girl sang Veronica's lament. Mingled with her pure, crystalline, emotional, flutelike voice was the low voice of a tall emaciated woman, anemic and pregnant. A little pot-bellied Por-tuguese and a gigantic black evangelist droningly accompanied the two women. After every stanza, the hunchbacked girl showed the crowd a white sheet bearing an impression of the miserable face of Our Saviour and the Negros would fall to their knees in a profusion of prayers and orations. While the procession got back under way and the jouncing candles made a fan-shaped pattern of little crosses with the bars of the window on the ceiling of the cell, my man said dully: 'Here's the weapon. Take my knife as a souvenir of your visit. For twenty years I've used it to cut my food in the prison mess-hall.' Then, with a long sigh, he added: 'You write for the newspapers. If you ever write about me, be sure and tell your friends the poets that life is dangerous today and someone who acts must carry his act through to the end without a murmur.' Oh! All of you, crowds in the great cities who go to the movies every night, watch, pay atten-tion. This tree invading the screen is seventy-five meters high. Its crown blocks out the sky and its branches are a world of gamboling little monkeys and screeching parakeets. The fork of every limb bleeds when the sun rises; these are orchids and other parasitic, sul-furous flowers that catch fire. Notice the tiny white blotch at the foot of the tree on the right. It's me, big as a louse dressed in white. In the next shot you watch me grow larger until I loom over you. Still. Here I am in close-up. Here's the assassin's knife. I rip open a box of crackers. I cut myself a slice of venison. Since then, I cut my bread with it. I cut my books. My book. This book. Have you had time to notice my companion, poking at the campfire? His face is smoky black and his hands are swollen from the stings of the *carapates*. It's Santiago, captain of the cowboys, a Paraguayan revolutionary who took part in the famous cavalry raid so greatly admired by the Saumur cadets. He is my guide in this forest, and instructs me on the good and evil properties of the plants. 'This is the tree whose ashes we use for cannon powder when we don't have enough during war.' Then he retraces his steps. 'A single incision, you see, and the wine for celebrating mass pours out.' Two or three hours later he adds, 'With its sap or its resin we cure asthma and all stomach ailments.' Then, in the evening, in camp, before falling asleep, 'Its seeds are the sovereign remedy against enchantments. Whoever wears them around the neck or on the heart, without knowing it, resists all the demon's temptations.' Three days later he returns again to the subject, and confidentially reveals: 'If you pick that tree's first flower the last Friday of the month, on a moonless night, and you return home without having heard the wolf's howl or the wild dog's yapping, you will restore your wife's virginity while sleeping with her.' Santiago likes me, esteems me, treats me like an equal, passes me his maté pipe because I lost an arm in the war. He loans me his horse, his rifle, his lasso, and teaches me to throw the bolos; but he never introduces me to his wife because of this dangerous confidence. When I leave, he too gives me his knife as a souvenir, a knife that has taken forty-seven lives. 'I killed my first man at the age of thirteen,' he told me one day. 'They all died for questions of honor.' I put that knife in a jewel box. Oh pure philosophy!

PRAIA GRANDE, MARCH 15, 1926

# The ABCs of Cinema

Cinema. Whirlwind of movement in space. Everything falls. The sun falls.[1] We fall in its wake. Like a chameleon, the human mind camouflages itself, camouflaging the universe. The world. The globe. The two hemispheres. Leibniz's monads and Schopenhauer's representation. My will. The cardinal hypotheses of science end in a sharp point[2] and the four calculators cumulate. Fusion. Everything opens up, tumbles down, blends in today, caves in, rises up, blossoms. Honor and money. Everything changes. Change. Morality and political economy. New civilization. New humanity. The digits have created an abstract, mathematical organism, useful gadgets intended to serve the senses' most vulgar needs and that are the brain's most beautiful projection. Automatism. Psychism. New commodities. Machines.[3] And it is the machine which recreates and displaces the sense of direction, and which finally discovers the sources of sensibility like the explorers Livingston, Burton, Speke, Grant, Baker, and Stanley, who located the sources of the Nile. But it is an anonymous discovery to which no name can be attached. What a lesson! And what do the celebrities and the stars matter to us! A hundred worlds, a thousand movements, a million dramas simultaneously enter the range of the eye with which cinema has endowed man. And, though arbitrary, this eye is more marvelous than the multifaceted eye of a fly. The brain is overwhelmed by it. An uproar of images. Tragic unity is displaced. We learn. We drink. Intoxication.

Reality no longer makes any sense. It has no significance. Everything is rhythm, word, life. No longer any need to demonstrate. We are in communion. Focus the lens on the hand, the corner of the mouth, the ear, and drama emerges, expands on a background of luminous mystery. Already there is no need for dialogue, soon characters will be judged useless. At high speed the life of flowers is Shakespearean; all of classicism is present in the slow-motion flexing of a biceps. On screen the slightest effort becomes painful, musical, and insects and microbes look like our most illustrious contemporaries. Eternity in the ephemeral. Gigantism. It is granted an aesthetic value which it has never had before. Utilitarianism. Theatrical drama, its situation, its devices, becomes useless. Attention is focused on the sinister lowering of the eyebrows. On the hand covered with criminal calluses. On a bit of fabric that bleeds continually. On a watch fob that stretches and swells like the veins at the temples. Millions of hearts stop beating at the same instant in all the capitals of the world and gales of laughter rack the countryside in far-flung villages. What is going to happen? And why is the material world impregnated with humanity? To such a point! What potential! Is it an explosion or a Hindu poem? Chemistries knot into complex plots and unravel toward conclusions. The least pulsation germinates and bears fruit. Crystallizations come to life. Ecstasy. Animals, plants, and minerals are ideas, emotions, digits. A number. As in the Middle Ages, the rhinoceros is Christ; the bear, the devil; jasper, vivacity; chrysoprase, pure humility. 6 and 9. We see our brother the wind, and the ocean is an abyss of men. And this is not some abstract, obscure, and complicated symbolism, it is part of a living organism that we startle, flush out, pursue, and which had never before been seen. Barbaric evidence. Sensitive depths in an Alexandre Dumas drama, a detective novel, or a banal Hollywood film. Over the audience's heads, the luminous cone quivers like a cetacean. Characters, beings and things, subjects and objects, stretch out from the screen in the hearth of the magic lantern. They plunge, turn, chase each other, encounter each other with fatal, astronomical precision.[4] A beam. Rays. The prodigious thread of a screw from which everything is whirled in a spiral. Projection of the fall of the sky. Space. Captured life. Life of the depths. Alphabet. Letter. ABC. Sequence and close-up. *What is ever seen is never seen.*[5] What an interview! 'When I began to take an interest in cinematography, film was a commercial and industrial novelty. I've put all my energies into expanding it and raising it to the level of a human language. My only merit consists in having been able to find the first two letters of this new alphabet, which is still far from complete: the *cut-back* and the *close-up*,' David Wark Griffith, the world's foremost director declares to me.[6] 'Art at the movies? Great Art?' responds Abel Gance, France's foremost director, to a journalist who came to watch him at work in Nice. 'Perhaps we could have made it that from the beginning. But first we had to learn the visual alphabet ourselves, before speaking and believing in our power; then we had to teach this elementary language.' Carlyle wanted to trace the origin of the modern world back to the legendary founder of the city of Thebes, to Cadmus. As he imported the Phoenician alphabet into Greece, Cadmus invented writing and the book. Before him, writing, mnemonic, ideographic, or phonetic, was always pictorial – from prehistoric man to the Egyptians, from the drawings that grace the walls of stone-age caves to hieroglyphics, the hieratic, traced on stone tablets, or the demotic, painted on ceramics, by way of the pictographs used by Eskimos and Australian aborigines, the Red Skins' colorful tattoos and the embroidery on Canadian wampum, the ancient Mayans' decorative quipus and the burls of the forest tribes of central Africa, the Tibetan, Chinese, and Korean calligrams – writing, even cuneiform writing, was above all else an aid to memory, a memorial to a sacred initiation: autocratic, individual. Then comes the black marketeer Cadmus, the magus, the magician, and immediately writing becomes an active, living thing, the ideal democratic nourishment, and the common language of the spirit. FIRST WORLD REVOLUTION. Human activity redoubles, intensifies. Greek civilization spreads. It embraces the Mediterranean. Commercial conquest and the literary life go hand in hand. The Romans engrave their history on copper or pewter plates.

There's a library in Alexandria. The Apostles and the Holy Fathers write on parchment. Propaganda. Finally, painting interpenetrates the Christian world and, during the fourteenth century, Jan van Eyck of Bruges invents oil painting. Adam and Eve, naked. SECOND WORLD REVOLUTION. In 1438, Korster prints with wood blocks in Harlem. Six years later, Jean Gensfleisch, known as Gutenberg, invents the mobile letter, and thirteen years later Schoeffer casts that letter in metal. With Caxton, printing intensifies. There is a deluge of books. Everything is reprinted and translated, the monastic missals and the writings of the ancients. Sculpture, drama, and architecture are reborn. Universities and libraries proliferate. Christopher Columbus discovers a new world. Religion splits in two. There is much general progress in commerce. Industry constructs boats. Fleets open up faraway markets. The antipodes exist. Nations are formed. People emigrate. New governments are founded on new principles of liberty and equality. Education becomes democratic and culture refined. Newspapers appear. The whole globe is caught in a network of tracks, of cables, of lines – overland lines, maritime lines, air lines. All the world's peoples are in contact. The wireless sings. Work becomes specialized, above and below. THIRD WORLD REVOLUTION. And here's Daguerre, a Frenchman, who invents photography. Fifty years later, cinema was born. Renewal! Renewal! Eternal Revolution. The latest advancements of the precise sciences, world war, the concept of relativity, political convulsions, everything foretells that we are on our way toward a new synthesis of the human spirit, toward a new humanity and that a race of new men is going to appear. Their language will be the cinema. Look! The pyrotechnists of Silence are ready. The image is at the primitive sources of emotion. Attempts have been made to capture it behind outmoded artistic formulas. Finally the good fight of white and black is going to begin on all the screens in the world. The floodgates of the new language are open. The letters of the new primer jostle each other, innumerable. Everything becomes possible! The Gospel of Tomorrow, the Spirit of Future Laws, the Scientific Epic, the Anticipatory Legend, the Vision of the Fourth Dimension of Existence, all the Interferences. Look! The revolution.

**A** *On location*
The camera which moves, which is no longer immobile, which records all levels simultaneously, which reverberates, which sets itself in motion.

**B** *In the theaters*
The spectator who is no longer immobile in his chair, who is wrenched out, assaulted, who participates in the action, who recognizes himself on the screen among the convulsions of the crowd, who shouts and cries out, protests and struggles.

**C** *On earth*
At the same time, in all the cities of the world, the crowd which leaves the theaters, which runs out into the streets like black blood, which extends its thousand tentacles like a powerful animal and with a tiny effort crushes the palaces, the prisons.

**Z** *Deep in the heart*
Watch the new generations growing up suddenly like flowers. Revolution. Youth of the world. Today.[7]

Paris, November 7, 1917   Rome, April 21, 1921

Cover of *La fin du monde filmée par l'Ange
Notre-Dame,* designed by Fernand Léger.
Monique Chefdor Collection. Photograph
by Yvonne Leenhardt. Gift from her film
archives.

# The End of the World Filmed by the Angel of Notre Dame

## Pro Domo

Beneath the R.A.F.'s raids, the bombardments and the systematic destruction of German cities, what happened, I wonder, to the Casanova manuscripts which the publisher Brockhaus has held in his strongbox in Leipzig since 1802, and which he didn't want to remove from their safekeeping when I came to see him in 1919, even though, at La Sirène, we were preparing the twelve-volume edition of the Chevalier de Scingalt's *Memoires*, the original manuscripts of which (written in a macaronic French) are still unpublished, despite our care and effort and the erudition of an international team of men of letters and bookworms, English, French, Danish, Italian, Austrian, and German, who devoted ten years of labor and patient research to verifying and commenting on each of the adventures recounted in these unbelievable *Memoires*, not allowing a single detail of the seductive Venetian's turbulent life to remain in obscurity, studying his speech, his actions, his gestures – I wonder what happened to Casanova's illegible manuscripts under the R.A.F.'s raids.

When I left my position as director of the Editions de la Sirène, the monumental edition of Casanova's work was well on the road to completion, and the first volume had just come off the presses (1924).

I had toiled like a slave at the technicalities of setting this vast undertaking in motion.

I consider the *Memoires* the true Encyclopedia of the eighteenth century, filled with *life* as they are, unlike Diderot's, and the work of a single man, who was neither an ideologue nor a theoretician: Casanova, who knew everyone, people and things, the way of life in all classes of society throughout all the countries of Europe, the roads, inns, brothels, gaming houses, chambermaids, bankers' daughters, and the Empress of Russia for whom he had invented a calendar, the Queen of France whom he had interviewed, the actresses and opera singers, Casanova, who was viewed as a dangerous swindler by the police, and passed in the salons for a superb gambler or sorcerer, the brilliant Chevalier de Seingalt, knight of industry, who frequented the working classes, craftsmen, seamstresses, salesgirls, people of the streets, coachmen and water carriers, with whom he chatted as intimately as with the Prince de Ligne or the Count de Salmour, who was dying with impatience to read the next chapter of the *Memoires,* though they were not yet published but circulated under cover and by rapid couriers who galloped across Europe (and since then the public has never had enough of them!), the man extemporizing the role of writer at the age of sixty to fill up his leisures as librarian in the deserted Bohemian castle of the Count de Wallenstein de Dux, where evenings and winter nights were longer than Scheherazade's thousand and one nights, and where the *bon vivant,* feeling himself growing old in solitude despite the library's twenty-five thousand volumes, relived his flickering life, blackening the pages of notebooks, throwing another log on the fire, and I think the fate of his work, which has become one of the world's great books, is extraordinary, for the old man was in no way a person of letters nor a master of language, and the version of the *Memoires* we know is neither the original text nor even a faithful translation or a moralizing arrangement or a selection of the best extracts or a piquant, erotic adaptation, which is a unique case in the history of world literature for a book which has become preferred bedside reading, and proves that in spite of the opinions of psychologists, moralists, historians, professional men of letters and others like them, there is no need for style, grammar, spelling, science, ideas, religion, or even any particular conviction to write an immortal book, and that personality and love of life will suffice, as well as the sheer amusement of writing – without pretension and for the sole pleasure of it – true stories.

A comforting example indeed when one thinks of the ambition of a Swinburne or the dog's life led posthumously by so many other Immortals who took themselves for writers and took Sky and Earth as witnesses of their genius, and who intrigued ceaselessly throughout their lives to get into the Academy! Casanova even escaped the ascendancy of professors, theses, and the university, which is why he is an incomparable educator of the young, who will always love him, for the young will always love life and love, women and wine, adventures and success, insubordination and gambling, mixing with the riffraff and the elite, questions of honor which require a seed of madness, an undertaking as desperate as the escape from the Venetian jail, money thrown out the window, a well-exercised body and the spirited if unscrupulous enjoyment of it, and since our handsome adventurer did not write in any admissible language, he cannot be claimed by any nation to be officially deformed or reformed. Casanova always took his chances, and still does . . .

Besides the monumental edition of the *Memoires,* I had prepared two hundred and one volumes when I turned my back on La Sirène, all ready for the presses, and which were published, or were not, in the collections of Tracts, Anthologies, Poets of Today, Short Mystical Writings, Novels of Alexandria, Novels of Byzantium, Painters' Sketchbooks, The Musical Siren, translations (Stevenson), reprints (Villon, Nerval, Baudelaire, Lautréamont, Apollinaire), unpublished texts (Mallarmé, Radiguet). I had turned my back. I had turned the page. I had left for Brazil. I was making movies. I was hunting. I was traveling. I was wandering. I was wasting my time. I was breathing, I was living, and the hell with libraries! And the books I had abandoned to the good or bad graces of La Sirène? I didn't give them another thought . . .

Among those books was the scenario of *The End of the World* on which I was counting to make my fortune, but . . . *habent sua fata libelli*.

A publisher should be an astrologist!

BLAISE CENDRARS

Saint-Segond, January 27, 1949

# 1
## Neutral God

1

It is December 31. God the Father is seated at his American executive desk. He is hurriedly signing countless pieces of paper. He is in shirt sleeves, with a green lampshade over his eyes. He gets up, lights a large cigar, glances at his watch, walks nervously through his office, pacing up and down as he chews at his cigar. He sits back down at his desk, feverishly pushes away the papers he has just signed, and opens the Great Book which is at his right. He examines it briefly, notes some figures in pencil on his memo pad, blows at the ashes fallen from his cigar between the pages of the book. Suddenly he grabs the telephone and dials furiously. He is convening his departmental supervisors.

2

Enter the departmental supervisors. The Pope, the Grand Rabbi, the Chief of the Orthodox Ecumenical Council, the Grand Master of the Masons, the Dalai Lama, the Great Bonze, the Reverend Pastor, the Christian Socialist Deputy, Rasputin, etc. They file in one after the other and line up behind the boss's chair. They all wear the emblems of their respective ministries, and have their account books in hand. God the Father calls each one of them in turn. Each one steps forward and presents his book, which God countersigns after having noted the total in his notebook. Then he dismisses them all with a brusque gesture.

## 3

Once he is alone, God the Father rapidly totals up the figures. It has been a good year. The Great War is yielding well. So many services for the repose of so many souls. One hundred thousand deaths at 1.25 francs each. He rubs his hands together joyously. But it can't go on forever. Costs are rising. He must think of something else. It's a good thing that . . .

A telegram is brought in to him:

MARS-CITY — P.K.Z. 19'18'43

COME. YOUR PRESENCE NECESSARY. FIRST PROPAGANDA PARADE FRIDAY 13TH. SUCCESS GUARANTEED.

MÉNÉLIK

He takes his hat, gloves, and cane and hurries out.

## 4

God the Father gets into his limousine. We see the new, flat, rectangular barracks of the GriGri's Communion Trust Company, Ltd., whose immense neon sign illuminates the twilight. It is evening. Millions of employees leave the office buildings. A busy crowd. Indescribable commotion. Hustle and bustle. Congestion. An infinite variety of costumes. Monks, Levites, popes, seminarists, clergymen, missionaries, and novices are clerks in the offices where lovely little nuns are typists.

## 5

Interlaken. Mars station. Immense buildings twinkle at the foot of the Jungfrau. Factories are everywhere on the mountain. Industrial housing. Derricks. Smoke stacks. Gigantic water pipes. Bridges, crosspieces, cables, pylons, reservoirs. The snorting of factories in the valley. The interplanetary train arrives in a tremendous uproar and falls into a magnetic net stretched from peak to peak. Elevators move up and down. Powerful projectors are switched on. Light signals. Optical telegraphy in color. The outbound train is pulled back, then hurled by the catapult of the giant dynamos. A flash of ultraviolet lightning. A spiral unwinds. The train has left. We see its taillights disappearing into the starry sky. The light signals intensify.

## 2
## The Barnum of Religions

6

Mars-City.

God the Father has set himself up on Mars, the Barnum of religions. The weekly cavalcade leaves the enclosure of the circus and falls into line.


7

From Krishna to Jesus, all founders of ancient religions file past. Then come General Booth, Herr Rudolf Schreiner, the Sar Péladan.[1] On large golden floats shaped like Gothic cathedrals, pagan temples, pagodas, synagogues, etc., the Christian Scientists, Methodists, Mormons, Anabaptists, etc. – all the modern sects celebrate their incomparable rites. African, Oceanic and Mexican fetishes. Grimacing masks. Ritual dances and chants. In cages, the evil deities, Asmodeus, Ahriman, etc., or certain phenomena such as Ahasurerus, the Visitandine Marie Alacoque, Huysmans, etc. Then several *tableaux vivants* or historic reconstructions such as: the Massacre of the Albigensians; the blue Bacchus, god of the apes; the flight of Mohammed, etc. Dust, banners, tapers, baldachins, a rain of confetti. Smoke from censers and incense burners. Harnessed elephants trumpet, leashed leopards scream. Camels, dromedaries, mules festooned in red. Here and there in the procession, a few charlatans: the fire-swallowing Zulu; the Man with a dog's head; Kekseksa, the wild woman who devours live chickens; Charlie Chaplin on stilts.

## 8

The crowd of Martians hurries ahead of the cavalcade. We see them in the soap bubbles that are their habitats, like imponderable fetuses in jars. They scintillate, chameleonlike, changing color according to the emotions that stir them.

## 9

The spells, the garish advertisements, the jangling music, the whole ostentatious production, the gold of the costumes, the violence of the perfumes, the tragic horror of certain pageants, certain scenes, certain famous sacrifices, all of the brutally sensual means exploited in this parade of religions, the sickening exhibition of certain martyrs – torture, for example, as it was inflicted on animals in Egyptian reincarnation – the frozen dread of the African masks, the cruelty of the dances, all of it agitates, dismays, and frightens the crowd of delicate, fragile Martians. God the Father has overshot his goal. Barnum is too vulgar.

## 10

We see the Martians' habitats radiating with violent, extreme colors. A few turn black, burst.

The bubbles begin to quiver. They seem to boil. We see them pile on top of each other, swell up immoderately or shrivel, flaccid. They flee.

## 11

The Martians release their police. We see bronze automatons, heavy and terrible, charging the procession. General disorder. The procession breaks up. God the Father flees into the desert.

# 3
## The Prophecy Gimmick

### 12

The City of Adventurers, in the human compound on Mars.

God the Father arrives, exhausted, ragged, bald. He's lost his collar, and his patent-leather shoes are ruined. He goes straight to the Grand Hotel, where his faithful Ménélik welcomes him.

### 13

The next morning.

God is in his bathrobe, sitting in an armchair. The colony's most influential members come to offer their condolences on the events of the previous day.

God announces that he intends to start a movie theater, and that he owns the greatest war movies ever made.

He is then informed that the Martians are staunch and undeceived pacifists. Iodine-eaters, they nourish themselves on the peptonic vapors of human blood, but they cannot bear the sight of the least cruelty.

God perseveres. He has plans, ideas, he doesn't want to abandon the game now. The spectacle of war unleashed on earth is too grandiose to resist. He must take advantage of it, profit from it.

Everyone gives him advice.

When they have all left, Ménélik approaches God and, in the manner of a respectful and admiring servant who permits himself to offer his master some advice, he suggests that the prophecies be fulfilled. God telegraphically convenes a few aged rogues from the Old Testament.

He rubs his hands together and smiles.


14

Enter the Prophets.

God describes his plan to fulfill the prophecies. Immediately each is defending and advocating his own. Cries, quarrels, gesticulations. Jews pulling each others' beards.

Nahum, Amos, and Micah, the three minor prophets of the canon, are particularly violent.[2] God takes them by the shoulders and pushes them all out the door.


15

Ménélik reenters and shows him a photograph of Notre-Dame de Paris, with the Angel perched at the peak between the two towers, his trumpet in hand. He explains that it is Thouroulde, the French poet who so valiantly sounded Roland's horn. He tells him that he is just what he needs. God acquiesces. He sends a coded message to the Angel of N.-D.

## 4
## The Angel of N.-D.: Cameraman

16

Paris. Panoramic view.

The Wheel; the Tower, Sacré-Coeur; the Pantheon; the Bridges. Upstream and downstream, the woods of Boulogne and Vincennes. The sunny slopes of Saint-Cloud and Montmorency. In the background, near Alfortville, the Seine streams up, luminous. Trains.

17

Characteristic scenes of the various *quartiers*. The artists in Montparnasse; the coquettes in the Bois; an aperitif at the Moulin-Rouge. Les Halles at five in the morning. A traffic jam at Châtelet; the Stock Exchange; the end of the day for the high fashion ateliers in the rue de la Paix; a society tea. Automobiles in the Place de l'Etoile, moving like pens. A strike at Villette. The *Matin*'s rotating presses; the Boulevard de l'Hôpital's welfare soups; the rue de la Glacière; the Luxembourg Gardens; the Quartier de l'Europe.

Flea markets, Quai de Grenelle. An operation at the Saint-Louis Hospital; large factories in the suburbs, etc.

18

Intimate scenes of Parisian interiors and streets.

The fruit vendor; the street peddler; the poet in the attic; the gentleman burglar; the great Marcelle. A man of the boulevards; the prisoner in cell 11. The sewer worker; the last Bohemian; old mother 'Keep Trimming' and old mother 'Specks'; the deacon of Saint Séverin, Monsieur Deibler; the messenger boy from the offices of the Ministry of Finance, etc.

19

Notre-Dame de Paris from all angles.

Minute details of its architecture. The chimeras. The apostles on the roof. And we see the Angel of N.-D. lifting his trumpet to his mouth.

## 5
## The End of the World

### 20

Noon. The square in front of Notre Dame. Buses circulate around the central refuge. A hearse leaves the Hôtel-Dieu followed by blind veterans. A division of municipal guards is lined up in front of the barracks across the way. Busy men cut across the square in all directions. On the left bank, a file of students moves past.

### 21

At the first blast of the trumpet, the disk of the sun grows a notch larger and its light weakens. All the stars appear suddenly in the sky. The moon turns visibly.

### 22

The Angel of N.-D. barely puffs out his cheeks.

### 23

We see passers-by covering their ears and turning their heads all the way around.

### 24

All the cities in the world rise on the horizon, slide down iron tracks, fall on top of each other, pile up in the square in front of Notre Dame.

25
The sun immobilizes. It is one minute past noon.

26
Instantly, everything that has been erected by men collapses onto those who are still alive and entombs them. Only those things that had a semblance of mechanical life last two seconds longer. We see trains still rolling with the last of their impetus, engines running in neutral, airplanes spinning downward through the sky.

27
An immense column of dust rises straight into the sky, then splits in two, divides, settles down, whirls into a vortex, thins out into threads, stretches in all directions; the winds blast; the sea opens and closes; the mountains of Mexico stumble in the light.

## 6
## High Speed and Slow Motion

### 28
With the death of man and the destruction of the domestic animals, the species and genera which had been hunted reappear. The seas are repopulated with whales and the surface of the earth is invaded by an enormous vegetation.

### 29
We see fallow fields greening and flowering furiously. An audacious vegetation blooms. Gramineae become fibrous, woody; weeds harden, tall and strong. Hemlock is leguminous. Shrubs appear, grow. The forests extend, and we see the plains of Europe darkening, uniformly blanketed with Appalachian shrubbery.

### 30
In the humid air, innumerable birds are flying, their plumage heavy and sticky. The otter and the beaver proliferate in the streams. Giant insects hatch in the swamps and lay their eggs, tirelessly.

### 31
The sun's disk wanes and cools again. Glaciers increase in height and expanse. We see the vicuña descending from the mountains of

the South, the condors and the bears. All of them take refuge in the steppes of the far North, where a current of warm air circulates. Everything adapts to the new environment of expanse and immensity. The vicuña's legs and neck elongate. The condor folds in its wings and controls its temper. The bear grows taller, swells, peels, becomes enormous. We see a giraffe, an iguanodon, a mammoth.

32
Then everything freezes.

The ice spreads; it invades the seas and the sky is weighted with it. The birds and the land animals are dead. On the banks of a narrow channel of tepid water, which alone remains, legless, humid beings with human faces and exterior lungs on both sides of their heads come to breathe.

33
Again the sun enlarges and its heat increases, and we see an intense and colorful island appearing through the curtain of mists. There, in slow motion and in a strange confusion, we see the shapes of all the annihilated beings: kangaroos hop by; lemurs fly; in its death-agony the duck-billed platypus comes to the foreground and looks at us with mocking eyes; the lyre-bird performs its sexual dance; the tubercular orangutan coughs; an armadillo rolls itself into a ball.

34
The desert. Bleached bones and immense eggshells.

35
It rains. It rains. Everything melts. Everything dissolves. The sky and the earth. The sun drools. It stretches out in the turbulent clouds and falls with them into the mud. We see its rays decomposing in drops of water and tiny rainbows seed the earth.

36
The sun is now very close. Its disk takes up one-quarter of the sky. It releases great bursts of fire perpendicular to the ground. Then it

steadies and rises a little and condenses into a thick, slightly ovoid, mass.

37
The glaciers are liquefied. The sun solidifies. The vapors thin out, rise halfway up. It is hot. A river of mud sweeps along huge peat bogs which agglomerate, fuse, and little by little form a continent. A sudden grass springs up to insane heights, wilts immediately, and revives. The flora of the coal mines grows, enlarges, spongy, mono-cellular, fleshy, and transparent.

38
We see the vascular plants harnessing the energy of the three ele-ments, transforming it, manufacturing complex substances which become nourishment.

39
It rains. It rains. The water rises. The needles of the conifers ramify, their tips flatten, they open out into umbels. Fungi grow on all the branches, floating with the current. Algae, yeasts, black sponges. Debris of all kinds accumulate at the bottom of the lakes. Plesio-sauria in decomposition.

40
The sun has dissolved. Something like a grainy and phosphorescent fog on a decomposed sea where a few obscene, giant, tumid larvae move heavily.

41
An obscure eye closes on all that has been.

42
A finger extends, lengthens, touches, probes, retracts, disappears in-side a conch. Tufts of grassy limbs awaken, turn like sunflowers. A stomach travels to the end of a thread and vibrates. Suctions,

spasms, airholes. Everything is blind under the water and the light is one-eyed.

### 43

The joint petrifies. The sated stomach becomes coral. Oxidizes. The pores emit a vitreous sweat. Movement, rarefied, freezes into a hinge. Life takes root and descends like a sounding line, anchors itself. In the deep, it is absolute night and only the stones are animated.

### 44

We see the crystallizations forming, stars with six branches, and each branch knots, crosses, in an X, a tau, a potent cross, a crosslet, a papal cross. This has no proportion on the screen. An infinitely small becomes infinitely big. The central fire projects the molecular shadow.

### 45

Polyhedrons evolve strategically. Colored gases precipitate. The complete minerals amalgamate, and we see the chemically pure elements gushing out of the slag heap of matter.

### 46

Everything is black.

We see a veined network of dark red fire sketch the family tree of the earth. It is dense like a nervous system.

### 47

A circulation is established, a boiling, a radiance. Sections of shadow are detached. Spindles of fire isolate themselves. Cones, cylinders, pyramids. Everything collapses into the central hearth. Explosion. And the burning sea rushes, torrential foam.

### 48

A ball.

The cracked, slashed, dessicated surface is scratched by the fingernail of a cold light. Peeling off from it, like skin, are layers of chalk, plaster, gypsum, then a layer of flint which strikes off sparks at the shock. Each geological epoch reappears. Craters are hollowed out. Pumice stone is lodged at the bottom of a cirque. Perpendicular slate. Rock. Granite. Borax. Hollow salt.

49
Everything spurts out. Everything merges. Tohu. Bohu. The oily sea, heavy like asphalt. The blackened, bloody earth liquefies. The waters become mountains and the continents rot.

Whirlwind.

50
Fin of a shark, the last ray of light slashes across chaotic space . . .

# 7
## Backward

**51**

In the projection room, Abin, who is in charge of running the magic lantern, sets fire to the mechanism. A fuse blows. A spring snaps. And the film runs vertiginously backward.

**52**

The last ray of light sets fire to the oily sea. The blackened earth blows up. Blocks of incandescent material drop straight down. Subterranean water vaporizes. Submarine land explodes. Water, air, and fire separate. The Armorian highlands loom up from the ocean. Chemistries synthesize. Arborescent organs pierce the shadow, rise, enlarge. An eye opens, edged with sea foam. The sun is like a healing plant. Everything that emerges from the waters is nourished, swells, is saturated with granular heat. Everything crawls. Yeasts, algae, and fungi are active, spread. Suddenly, the giant fossils stand up. It rains. The vapors condense. The glaciers form. It is cold. The sun is now very pale. It retreats, grows into a disk, intensifies. The dust of the desert revives. A thousand legless animals slither in the sand. Then, everything freezes over. Ice floes. The sea lion screams and writhes. The elephant leaves the banks of a polar sea. Inland, the vicuña flees into the mountains. Everything dries out gently, plants and birds take on a very gentle greenish glow. Vegetables are appetizing. Sheep, cows, horses in the prairies.

## 53

We see Paris again. The trains, the circulating automobiles. The busy crowd in the square in front of Notre Dame. The weary gesture of the Angel of N.-D., taking the trumpet from his mouth.

## 54

A break in the film, then, after a long gap, God, fleeing from the Martians, leaving the desert, returning to the parade which returns to the enclosure of the circus, leaving Mars, arriving at Interlaken, walking backward toward his limousine, which drives in reverse to the offices of the GriGri's Communion Trust Co., Ltd. In his office, he puts down his gloves, hat, cane.

## 55

And we see, as in the beginning, God the Father, sitting at his American executive desk, chewing furiously on his cigar . . .

ETC.

Bankruptcy.

**The Eubage; or, At the Antipodes of Unity**

# 1

## On the Itinerary for Traveling to the Region of the Sky

After weighing anchor, we left the earth to enter the ocean of solar light which is our breathable atmosphere. Having reached its extreme limits, we resolutely embarked on the rapids of the ozone region. We were moving so quickly that we could not gauge our speed and it seemed to us that we were standing still. The Earth was invisible in our wake and in front of us the stars had ceased to exist. Finally we took the great plunge into the void, splashed with star foam. We tacked along the Great Bear for seven centuries by the clock, often passing beneath black rainbows; then, having rounded Cape Orion, we dove straight ahead into the South, which is the North of the sky.

We caught some interstellar beings and were dumbfounded by their strangeness, but we regaled ourselves on their exquisite flesh, which was a welcome addition to the crew's ordinary fare.

Everyone was in good spirits and in good health.

Following my men's example, I shook off the stupor which had engulfed me as I watched the success of this unexpected departure. I gave the order to hoist our great golden flag bearing the arms of Human Passion, and I looked through a porthole.

Here is what I saw as I emerged from the goose-flesh of my spirit:

59

## 2
## On the Eel, and On the Sponge Which Is the Bottom of the Sky

APRIL

Behind the Milky Way there is an Eel, a kind of Serpent of the Sky. It feeds on the suns that teem in the mire of the depths. Its eye is like the four-leaf clover of outer space, and at the end of its tail, like little bells, erupting worlds mark out time. When it sheds its skin, a comet falls from every scale. And the digestion of this being is Light. Like an earthworm in a root it is caught in the base of a sponge which it gnaws and which almost entirely conceals it. Every pore of this sponge breathes and groans like a human generation. This sponge is Sponge of the Shadows, Tuft of Tongues, Organ of Origins. Like a brain in a skull, it molds itself into the first form. It is the primary, the simplest, and the most elementary specimen of a family of inverted, unspeakable, and inadmissible beings, at the Antipodes of Unity.

6I

## 3
## On Musical Instruments

Every morning a transparent membrane stretches out across the horizon. The instant that an eyelid opens, a bud of anemone flesh blooms, a grain of sand or a sun comes to life, a fly, a human being, an animal or a plant trembles, or any force whatsoever embarks on its career, this ultrasensitive membrane vibrates, takes the sound in, makes it echo, amplifies it into a tremendous noise. Immediately, the mountain of Waters, which occupies all of the East of space, from zenith to nadir, collapses, and pours itself onto the mountain of Salt which is in the West. A circulation develops, a seething, a howling, a cyclone of sounds going from bass to shrill and then back down, in a vertiginous cadenza, to bass. At first, nothing can be distinguished; then you are dazzled by peculiar gleams, flashes, a glaring light. Shadows pass before your tired eyes, then fleetingly disappear, their white bellies flashing like fish in water. Elementary forms are defined: a square, an oval, a circle. They rise to the surface and burst like globules. Now everything wriggles with finlike movements, the square elongates, the oval hollows out, the circle breaks into a star; mouths, lips, throats; everything leaps into the void with a great cry; it all rushes in from every direction, gathers, heaps up, stretches out into the insane shape of a mastodon's tongue. This tongue jerks, labors, with unbelievable effort it stammers, speaks. It tells.

Then a great wind rises up which dissolves it, unravels it like a cloud; dew, cellos, harps, trumpets, and drums can be seen falling from it, immutable flowers which take root in every Sphere and which every spiritual being can pluck in the attempt to recreate the NORM.

# 4
## On the Great Joy of the Stars

JUNE

On the axis of Noon, the mouth of a grotto opens and startles you like a blue buttercup: inside, the meticulous progress of the planets can be watched. Nothing is as simple, grand, calm, and serene as this sight, nothing else releases so much happiness. A phonograph record that turns, but without anything mechanical. Chinese music. Up in Tibet, the sturdy gong of contemplation. In some rock crystals you see the ring of Venus like the neck of a black giraffe, speckled Jupiter, the jungle of Mars, Earth, inalterable as platinum.

In these meadows, breathing is a wild horse.

# 5
## On Honey

In the river of Time which flows in Space, lazy trout can be glimpsed among the luxuriant grasses. The water is clear, the current limpid. At the bottom, among the ultraviolet and infrared rays of decomposed light, we can see the foaming of the odomagnetic gems that make up the aeroliths. Metals, rocks and roots, grasses and all the leaves are rich with their own life. The vegetation is audacious. While flying over the river's source in this little valley today, with blasts of my cannon I hunted the enormous hybrid butterfly of the Summit of the Hours whose wings are isochronal: one is morning, the other evening. Our little harpoons would not catch on its diaphanous wings, and we had to discharge twenty-eight of them before we succeeded in hooking one in its belly. The mortally wounded animal plunged, forced itself up again, swerved, and fled with a great beating of its wings, pulling us in its wake, since the harpoon held well.

The giant insect rose, fell, bucked, somersaulted, spun around, tugging at us, carrying us, shaking us. At moments we found ourselves on top of it, in the radiance of its head, at other moments we were beneath it, in the night of its belly. Any of its thrashings could have capsized us, and so, fearing that we might lose our hold on it if the film were to break, I ordered our gunner to fire an explosive shell at the butterfly's eye. The explosion wreaked terrible damage. I saw the animal slide a long way and fall, its wings stiff. We fell behind it, spinning like a corkscrew.

The situation was critical. Our frail bark went into a nose dive. The engines were dead. The crew had all lost their balance and fallen to the floor. I alone remained standing, gripping the front porthole with a sharp pain in my head. And it was at that precise instant that I had a vision of the madness of our enterprise. My mind was overcome by the error of our discoveries and the inanity of our scientific endeavors.

We had been spiraling downward forever, between the evening and the morning. No, there are no laws; no, there are no measurements. There is no center. No unity, no time, no space. Our scientific reasoning is a poor little analytic instrument; a web of strands woven tighter and tighter which traps and binds the inert terms of our dialectic; a filter which strips words of any spirit, any image, any creative force, any knowledge, which isolates them, dissects them, washes them, purifies them, strips them of any tendrils, any particles, any scoria remaining from their birth, in order, finally, to circumscribe, to specify a thing which is unique and hence metaphysical, in other words, *nothing,* since everything holds together, is attached and repelled 'and you cannot define a blade of grass without taking apart the universe.'

And how could it take apart the universe, or define a blade of grass, this serous effusion in the brain which we call scientific reasoning, since science is ignorant of the most primary processes of the universe and does not know to what the amount of starch present in one blade of grass can be attributed: the composition of the soil? the effects of the climate? the degeneration of the seed? the method of cultivation?

No, the point does not exist, its definition can equally be used to define space (neither length, nor width, nor breadth), and all that it generates is mental fatigue, convention, dead letter, rho and phi. Without any superstition, the instinctive babbling of a child sum-

mons the universe, gathers it around his cradle and graciously offers
him its reality. Our senses speak and affirm. Physically, all is whim,
madness, habit, vice. All is depth. The universe is isomeric, which
means that it is entirely and everywhere composed of the same elements which, however, have properties which (entirely and everywhere) differ according to their situation.

How could I have entrusted my life and the lives of my companions to this fragile machine, constructed, I now admitted to myself,
blindly, tentatively? Had I not worked in the midst of incertitude
and continual doubt? Yes, I, the honest and conscientious man of
science, inventor of this prodigious engine which had transported
us into the sky, and of which I was rightfully proud, I, the man who
tamed the universal Spiral, as my fellow citizens had called me after
my definitive work on the life of numbers, was I not an impostor? I
had reduced geometry, trigonometry, applied and celestial mechanics, laws and theories which were the most scientific, the most certain, the most demonstrable, the most stable, to tabula rasa, in order
to adopt the most chimeric, the most insane, the most obscure hypotheses, like an inspired prophet, like a poet who talks or pretends
to talk nonsense.

How had I been able to persuade my companions to follow me?
Yes, why had they had faith in me when I myself no longer believed
in anything, when I struggled to conceal my madness? My bearing,
my authoritative gaze, and the millennial dream inspired by an intellectual forehead.

And when I thought all was lost, the need to control and direct,
which has always forced me to act, intervened obscurely. I glanced
out the porthole. The monster which was dragging us had just run
aground. We were only half a cable's length from it and we were
about to smash into it.

'Everyone to their posts!' I shouted in a thundering voice. I had
the cables which tied us to our prey blown up. Powerful electrical
discharges made the repulsite panels on our hull vibrate. The enormous rear turbine was reactivated. I managed to fix the apparatus by
hitting it with an iron bar, and with a terrible swerve our vehicle

came to a stop, hanging barely two meters above the giant carcass. My men looked at me, haggard. A nervous tic made me smile. But the quartermasters were crying 'All hands on deck!' Already, silent cranes were extending from the flanks of our vessel to begin dismembering the corpse. My passion returned. Feverishly I inventoried all the booty we were stockpiling.

This is what we found inside the dead butterfly:

1. Foaming ARIES, who hammered at its mutilated head.

2. Warm CANCER, smoldering in its breast.

3. Roaring LEO, headquartered in its solar plexus.

4. The GEMINI twins, straddling its antennae.

5. Raging TAURUS, spurting from its neck.

6. LIBRA, on the axis of its wings (which were too large to fit into the ship).

7. VIRGO, asleep like a human being in its flanks.

8. SCORPIO, gnawing at its stomach (he was the one hit by the harpoon).

9. SAGITTARIUS, who defended its mouth.

10. CAPRICORN at the knot of its thorax.

11 and 12. Rippling AQUARIUS and PISCES, who swam in its eyes.

Its nervous limbs clutched blindly at empty space, white as water lilies.

As I was exploring its proboscis, a drop of honey fell.

Life effectively, manifestly, and formally is space and time, sublimated, molten, perfumed. Honey.

**6**

**On the Place Where Old Moons Rest, On Wheat and On the Eye**

We had just taken off and were beginning to gain a little altitude when I was warned that a chain of mountains had been sighted in our wake. Immediately I went to the cartography center in the rear tower. Indeed, geometric summits could be distinguished on the horizon. I reversed our direction and we proceeded slowly toward the N.N.W.

Soon we entered an essentially luminous zone. We navigated through sparks, reflections, fool's gold. The radiations seemed to become palpable, to granulate and become sonorous. It sounded like a continuous slithering against our hull.

One of the more powerful rays crashed into us like a mortar shell and made our whole ship resonate; sometimes a wave seemed to lift it. The emissions of light succeeded each other more and more rapidly, densely, and violently, all of them coming from the mountains which barred our way. A spectral analysis determined the presence of osmium, and from this I concluded that the mountains we had in front of us were formed of fully active platinum; as we approached them, the interior hull of our engine, which was made of crystal, was polarizing. This explained our increasingly slow and arduous progress, as well.

In this difficult fashion, we arrived at a uniform, smooth, polished, and gleaming wall, the color of slate. Its edges were free of any nick or crevice. Having surmounted this wall, we discovered another inclined surface further along, just as uniform, smooth, polished, and gleaming. We went all the way around the mountain. It was one single block of platinum, an enormous and regular icosahedron. Twenty-nine more blocks of the same size and shape joined end to end made up this chain of mountains, which looked like a giant caterpillar of the processionary type. The last block was split down the center. We entered this narrow, deep, and sinuous canyon.

The opening was lined with a white, brittle metal that was crumbling; on the ground, traces of it gave off the attenuated colors of the rainbow.

Ahead, enormous concretions jutted out from the canyon walls and were broken off by our passage, raising reddish, brown, and saffron clouds behind us. Further along, at the bottom of a well, a thick, heavy, bloody spring flowed intermittently; floating in it were a kind of warm peat, bits of vegetation, flabby crystals, rubber stars, drooling rocks, animal syrup, congealed oil. The corridor ended in an immense cirque, where, in an aquatic twilight, a jumble of forms swam. The shadows of the objects chaotically overlapped and interpenetrated, hardly even opaque. Strange tumult! The last moon was molding in a porous basin, and all around old moons were scattered, lying filthy, pitiful, dull, untarnished, belly-up among a collection of the most heteroclite objects, the sort of things which usually confront each other in the wings of a theater, or in an inverted brain. We made an about-face in this enclosure, and before reentering the narrow corridor which had brought us there I had the search lights switched on. The old moons reanimated, pallid and ivory-colored, and I had a rapid and infinitely tragic vision of the elephant cemetery described by Sinbad the Sailor of the *Thousand and One Nights,* the great white carcasses, the heaps of bleaching bones!

Now we were nearing the mouth of the canyon. Seen from inside the mountain, the irradiations trembled at the luminous threshold like the lashes of an eyelid. In front of us, the entire field of vision palpitated, rippling out to infinity, a golden harvest, the fragrance of light's most beautiful grains. In passing, I reaped a few of the heaviest stalks. I bound them into a sheaf which I am bringing back with me to seed man's Earth for eternity.

POLARIS, called *Szarawka* or *Polish* wheat: yellow grain, very particular and characteristic. White straw of average height, not easily crushed. Resists frost very well.

ALGOL, called *Valette Red:* red grain, large, plump, and heavy. Reddish straw, of average height, slender, resists crushing. Ripens early, has little subsidiary growth, does well on almost any terrain. Can be planted until the end of February.

ALTAIR, called *Japhet* or *God's* wheat: lovely reddish grain, plump, ripens well. White straw of average height, quite strong. Adapts to every terrain. To be planted in autumn and spring. Ripens early. No subsidiary growth.

BETELGEUSE, called *Good Farmer:* heavy, yellow grain, much appreciated by millers, resistant to rust. Light yellow straw, short and thin. Ripens early, little subsidiary growth, does well on almost any terrain.

THE SPIKE, called *Red Scotch Goldenrod:* average grain, usually glossy, half red, half yellow. Very beautiful red straw, tall and strong, often violet-colored below the spike. Very hearty, resists frost and diseases. Very good subsidiary growth. Ripens late.

ALDEBARAN, called *Meadow* wheat: large, magnificent grain, light yellow and heavy. Lovely white straw, quite tall, but very resistant. Doesn't rust or sunburn. Good subsidiary growth. Succeeds on any terrain.

RIGEL, called *Carter:* yellowish-gray grain, very large, a bit wrinkled. White straw, tall, but heavy and uncrushable. Average subsidiary growth. Ripens early. Needs a good terrain.

ARCHEMARD,[1] called *Yellow Beard:* red-brown grain, black at the seed. Yellow straw. Brown spike, velvety, and enormous. The most productive of all the varieties. Very hearty. Good subsidiary growth. Resistant to frost and diseases. Its faults are ripening late and being difficult to thresh.

THE SOUTHERN CROSS, called *Reed:* white grain, fairly large, very resistant. Large leaves. The earliest of all the square-stalked varieties. Ripens well. Should be sown in good earth.

I have come to believe that we were traveling through an eye, and that I harvested gazes. Wheat of the brain.

## 7
## On the Parturition of Colors

Where are we? Everything is becoming lighter, dissolving. The machine barks. Every revolution of the turbine is my most intimate thought.

Advance! Flee! Full speed ahead! The crystal shell buckles, becomes malleable. The best amalgamations melt. Liquids are volatilized. The air is becoming unbreathable. My men fall prey to a dismayed laughter. I have had to tie them up, one by one, attaching their hands to the controls, immobilizing them at their posts. Will the automatism of their gestures save us?

Earlier, as I made my rounds, the floor gave way beneath my weight; I sank into the deck of the ship as if it were marshland. The hardest substances shed tears of heat. The radiant globes are misted over. Polished angles rust. Burnished surfaces tarnish. The luminous dials are going out. Everything around me is cracking. Everything disintegrates, melts, swoons, becomes immaterial.

I have taken refuge in the central cabin. I have insulated it. I seize the coffer which contains the agent, the principle of my engine: the molecular Spiral. Come what may! My eye clamped to the coffer's periscope, I observe the perpetual motion of which I am the inventor. Here is the spark. One millionth of a second. A spark oscillates, palpitates, lives, progresses through an absolute void, enclosed in a yellow hepatite.[2] All around, the Zn vibrios, which ought to be capturing, decomposing, and multiplying the point of ultrawhite incandescence, rear up, standing, saturated, a short circuit blunting their points. Nothing works now. The void produced by the hepatite is invading every one of the machine's organs. Every body, every object, every instrument on board dilates, then shrivels up, sinks into itself, lights up with a thousand vermicular slits. The intramolecular network can be distinguished and the atoms revolve visibly. My ship opens like the rose of the winds and closes like a capsule. We are about to explode. I live now only by my brain! I must perform hemospasia.[3] My fingers at the keyboard of the void, I strain to divert the flood of vacuum into the parts of the engine that are vacuum ballasts. Enormous discharges of vacuum reestablish the coefficient of density. I then witness a strange phenomenon. In the returning flame, the hepatite sputters. Everything smokes. My field of vision is submerged in a whirlwind. A brownish red invades the screen little by little and fills it. A dark, rugged red, wrinkled like kelp, made of slats placed side by side. Each slat is tipped by a pustule which quivers and bursts like cooling lava. Suddenly, the mass of fucus red separates down the middle. The slats are grouped to the right and to the left. The activity of the pustules redoubles. A blue stripe appears which rapidly widens and extends up and down. The frondescent blue branches out in all directions. Tiny, trembling leaves, quince-shaped like the leaflets of maidenhair fern, grow against the red. The red slats and the blue leaflets, alternating two by two, gently revolve and vanish. There remain only two blotches shaped like stringbeans, one red, the other blue, confronting each other. They look like two embryos, masculine and feminine. They move toward each other, connect, break apart, and reproduce by cells and clumps of cells. Each spore, each sporocarp, is surrounded by a violet thread which quickly enlarges, swells, and, like a pistil, becomes fleshy. Small orange lozenges marble its surface. The lozenges are visibly growing. Soon the orange and the violet devour each other, rip each other apart. Branches, limbs, and trunks

76

all tremble, lie down, rise up. Suddenly the orange blooms like a pumpkin blossom. The calyx hollows out. At the bottom, two violet pistils tremble against a red stamen. The disk enlarges by a notch. Everything turns vertiginously from the center to the periphery. A ball is forming, colored the most dazzling yellow. It looks like a fruit. The yellow explodes. Multicolored pits shoot out, seeds of many different shapes, confetti. Then everything falls, from high to low, as dense as hail, uniformly green. Threads are traced, chains, bonds. Twigs, stems. Knotted, slender, climbing. This pasture tans and grows gray to disappear little by little in a haze of evanescent forms melting into white. The white steadies, hardens, freezes. An ultrawhite disk. At the center, the spiral is functioning. Its motion is regular. The liquids are there, irrepressible. The harder substances have sharp edges, neat angles. The domestic forms develop one from another, familiar and useful. The rudder obeys. My lovely ship appears to me as the mathematical fruit of volume.

Matter is color in space, the fall into the void, and we have industrialized it. This is the Origin.

## 8
## On the Heteroclite

Above, below, the Sky seizes us from everywhere.

We are sailing through something soft, calm, and tender. Jumbled constellations move past us like white clouds in a summer sky. Soapy masses rise and fall, dive, slide, tilt. Everything is comfortable. In our wake, it is snowy.

We are moving less and less quickly. Everything thickens. Little by little I realize we are in the Baltic, the Baltic of the Sky. The gentle shimmer of mother-of-pearl. Bits of down float by. A whirlwind of wings.

Snowflakes are fluttering, lightly.

Now we are making barely three knots an hour, penetrating a resistance, a flaccid barrier full of hoarse barks, agitated fins, the rasp of scales.

I believe that we have reached a dead end. For the first time I think of the human region we left behind. My men, pale, bloodless, anemic, a blue tint beneath their skin and melancholy in their gestures, their gazes. The clock, the clock spins frantically in reverse, 1,000 years, 10,000 years, 100,000 years. We are on our way. What have we found? A giant penguin snickers and flaps its wings. My index finger is like a beak under a wing, grooming my wrinkles. The sky is a gelatinous oil, streaked with yellow, curdled with carnelian, oil frozen in a green bottle. We are at the bottom.

Everything wriggles, opening and shutting like gills. Minuscule mouths. Round, bulbous things disappear, come, go, reveal themselves, melt into a scintillation. The gilded balls rise, fall, trace out figures. Meditation? Game? Arabesques and designs can be perceived. A herd of piebald horses bolts. Prairie dogs bark. A chimpanzee swings from one arm. The palm tree bends. A swarm of butterflies. A cluster of birds. A small basset hound. A caterpillar. A mole, spotted like a peacock.

A clown's laughter. The embroidery is torn. The emerald stagecoach topples over. Everything shatters. Everything breaks. Transparent craters open and reveal a gleaming array of kitchen utensils made of the very best copper. An Indian and a blue Negro dance around the hearth and juggle large Spanish onions. An ostrich egg hurtles down a slope. Sheep are turning, dazed by vertigo, at the bottom of a funnel. Snowball. The avalanche disintegrates as it comes to a halt. A jet of water spurts from it, rigid. The crack of a whip. Lightning. The blizzard. Forests grow and are chopped down. Shards of ice take flight like tiles. A woman shakes her skirts. The blades of windmills turn. In a tremendous slide, books fall off their shelves, open, and their pages whirl, above, below, like a flock of seagulls behind us.

Then everything becomes glassy, blurred, without depth, like an untoned photograph. Silver bath. A volley of mountains. We are caught in the ice field of the sky.

Winter vacation.

On the ice, I examine the Little Bear's frozen footprints, stupefied. In the middle is the hole where the seal of black Night comes to breath.

To escape from the melancholy which is overcoming me, I bury myself once more in Rob's principal work, *Fludd de Fluctibus Armigero: Tractatus Secundus de Naturae Simia seu Technica macroscosmi historia in partes undecim divisa. Fol. In Nobile Oppenheimio 1618,* which is the most thorough treatise on the music of the Spheres.[4]

# 9
## On the Human Mind

*Spring*

We are driving on the shores of light. At the end, behind a dune, we come upon two young suns which tumble, somersault, and rip creation apart with their new teeth like two lion cubs. The dust of the four elements makes a mane around them that their boisterous mouths rip to shreds. Everything flies into pieces, the forests, the mountains; and they sharpen their young claws on the navel of the Universe.

# 10
## On Woman

It is the summer of Berenice. Hairs, cables, lianas, have seized us, are hoisting us to the center of such a strange forest of symbols! The nearest stars are like tropical flowers, and the farthest howl and bark like jackals or dogs. A monkey presses against the porthole of my cabin and I cannot avert my gaze from its congested face. Behind it, the pure light we have just left retreats into the distance, intensifies and subsides.

# 11
## On the Calendar

We are at the naked summit of space, the twin peak which is continuously collapsing, the double mountain of sand which flows like an hourglass, and which overturns and returns.

Down below, the Earth is, all at once, within our grasp, and seems very close. For the flicker of an eye, the gnarled rustic who leads it can be seen, and we hear his hoarse voice directing the oxen harnessed to the heavy plow. The first furrow marks the sky from one end to the other. Two hemispheres come apart. Everything falls. We roll, caught in the fall, dragged along. The night turns around, falls on us. The sand covers us. The ocean floor empties out onto us.

## 12
## On Projection Powder

The engine is rocking us like a cradle. We are entering the zone of attractions, gravitation, conjugations, calculations of Melancholy, and monograms of the Heart. The network of nerves and veins stands out against the unleavened wafer of night like a microscopic preparation.

Parabolas. Caroms.

Everything cools. Graphic beauty is muddled. This is old age which touches us unexpectedly, sudden and terrible like a comet. Is this 7? Is this 4? We cannot count on our fingers any more. My companions turn white from head to toe and fall into dust.

'Everyone to his post!'

There isn't even a skull to snicker. We will be agglomerated, digested, annihilated, thrown to the moray eels behind the sky. I cannot battle against the decomposition, but I can still control our direction. We must return to our home port. I believe I still have the force to return among men. I employ a small vaporizer. The projection powder transmutes our engine into pure solar matter. Nothing can stop us now; we are returning to our origin.

Already we are rising, we are falling vertiginously. We leave the picturesque tableau of the sky behind us – the chieftains, the slaves, the bazaar, the tattoos made for export – to greet in passing the most familiar astronomies, flying by in pairs.

Constellations in flocks like birds announce that we are nearing home. Here already is the great waterfall. I am fainting. I no longer have the strength to land. We speed through the human atmosphere like a meteorite. Golden scarab. Zigzagging like a question mark. Explosion.

Paris, Courcelles, Nice, & La Pierre

May 3–28, 1917; December 1917

*Si vous ne vous foutez
pas de la peinture,
elle se foutra de vous.*

[Don't give a damn
about painting or
painting won't give a
damn about you.]

Statement made by the
painter Louis David
to one of his students

# Painters

*For Madame Eugenia Huici de Errazuriz*

# 1
## MODERNITIES

**What Will Be the New Mode of Painting?** The Salon of the Independents will soon be opening, it has been announced. It will be an event to equal the most celebrated of the prewar openings. For the first time since the war,[1] every one of the younger generation's styles will be exhibited together. There is great commotion in the art world. Will 1919 also be a landmark year for painting?

The newcomers just back from the front are asking:

What will be the new mode of painting?[2] Will there be surprises? Sensations? Novelties? Has cubism come to an end? Will we see any examples of the young, revolutionary painting that is creating a furor in Russia? Will a new *-ism* be coined to designate the new beauty? Which critic will have the honor of giving the new movement its name, and which will be the first to laugh at it? For a new world, a new art . . .

The cube has disintegrated. A thousand new styles have emerged. There is a new beauty. The younger French poets are well aware of this, and they have already identified some of its elements: the universality and grandeur of modern life; the optimistic pessimism of the man of today; his passion, his frenetic intelligence, his reality; the fever of activity that shakes us all; travel, business, sports. The painters, in turn, are grappling with this prodigious depth. The formula, the cubist formulas, no longer suffice. Modern life's features and contrasts are too complex. You can't number them scientifically, nor can you capture them with any technique, however intellectual. First and foremost, the world's reality is a sensation. This is why the new painters are sensuous, and the new element they present to us is: color!

I predict, then, a great deal of color,[3] and a wholly new color.

But that is not all. This new color demands new forms; this pure color demands large sizes. For this reason, I predict many large canvases, canvases of enormous dimensions, and since large canvases demand a subject, I predict a renaissance of the subject.[4]

At last painting will make sense to us, for the subject is man. And man is you and I, at work or at play, with our familiar objects and ventures. I am not predicting a resurgence of portraiture but, rather, a new interpretation of man. We will recognize ourselves individually in the painters themselves,[5] who will have a way of feeling instead of a theory. This is why I do not believe there will be a new -ism. We will finally have painting, individual, idiosyncratic painting, and not theoretical, collective, anonymous painting. We will not say 'I went to see the -ists' but 'I like so-and-so's work.' And this is a great revolution. Finally we will have one painter and another painter: Mallarmé and Rimbaud.

PARIS, MAY 9, 1919

## 2
## MODERNITIES

**Who Will Their Masters Be?** Something has changed, there is something like a renewal in painting. Painters are searching for their identities, evolving. Some are leaving cubism to go the route of the *pompiers* again and to get stuck in it; others circle cubism, approach it at an angle, and get caught. The few shows organized before the war showed us these astonishing comings and goings. Groups disappeared as soon as they were formed. And there was a great waste.

However, these shows were not entirely useless. They demonstrated that the younger painters are in full effervescence; that they are eager to reject every recognized school, to leave behind every theory imposed on them so that they can enter the world of great painting, and boldly make their own discoveries. The independent spirit of today's young painters is pleasing and can only be encouraged. The young are serious; the young are thoughtful. Impatient as they may be, they do not go about rejecting everything pell-mell. They have made their choices among their immediate predecessors. Only a select few have been accepted. And if they don't venerate them enough to follow their teachings to the letter, they love them enough not to be afraid of consecrating them as 'masters' nor of choosing them from opposing schools and styles.

And this is today's big surprise. There will be a revaluation of the painting of the last fifteen years. And this revaluation will be carried out by the young painters who, in their choices, will give us not a rating of retrospective values but an indication of what will be appreciated by the painting of tomorrow. Unexpected spiritual filiations will thus be established; and quite a few painters who have been strangers to each other until now will be very surprised to find themselves united in the same esteem. In this way we can begin, starting today, to imagine what will lie beyond cubism.

We will grant recognition to all the elders who, however unknowingly, have assembled any of the elements of the violent beauty that possesses those of us who are young and that compels us: the beauty of the modern world.

PARIS, MAY 9, 1919

## 3
## MODERNITIES

**Why Is The 'Cube' Disintegrating?** Of all the avant-garde schools, one, only one, was able to hold on through the war, organize itself, and endure: the cubist school. The Gallery of Modern Effort[6] opened its doors to the cubists. It has already exhibited the works of Herbin, Laurens, Léger, Metzinger, Braque, Gris, Csaky, Sévérini, Picasso, Hayden, etc.

Taken together, these works leave one very clear impression: here, too, there has been a great deal of waste. Beneath an apparent unity, a thousand dissident styles are burgeoning. The formula, the cubist formulas, have become too rigid and can no longer contain the painters' personalities. Cubism is coming out of its anonymous phase. We are now allowed to use names. These names, which break up the collective 'cube,' are the first cause – an internal cause – of its disintegration. There are finally canvases which do not look alike, and which cannot be mistaken for each other. This is why, properly speaking, there is no longer a cubist school. I am acquainted with certain painters who have emerged from cubism and who, today, affirm their lofty personalities. As for the others, those still clinging to the 'cubist' label, they are falling further and further out of favor and will soon disappear beneath the school's debris. The day is already at hand when the term 'cubism' will have no more than a nominative value, designating, in the history of contemporary painting, certain investigations carried out by painters between 1907 and 1914. It would be inane not to recognize the importance of the cubist movement, as it was idiotic to laugh at it. But it is just as idiotic and inane to restrict ourselves to a doctrine which, today, marks a historic milestone, and to fail to recognize that cubism no longer offers enough novelty and surprise to continue to nourish a new generation.

It has lasted for ten years.

It is a phase we seem to have passed through.

The spirit of the generation returning from the front has been awakened by other problems and its investigations are moving in a new direction. Above all, the new generation is very much its own master. It wants to construct. And I do not think that it will get lost in long theoretical investigations, since it has some elements in hand: color. It will construct through color.

I am not writing a history of cubism or an exposition of its doctrines. For that, I refer the reader to the works which have discussed it, and which have demonstrated the lofty standards of this mode of painting. I will restrict myself here to a brief critique of cubism's first mistake, a theoretical mistake, which is, today, the second cause, an external cause, of the disintegration of the 'cube.'

What were the four principal theoretical concerns of the cubist painters?

1. The investigation of depth (reality, sur-reality, life);
2. The study of volumes (space);
3. The study of measures (time);
4. The critique and reappraisal of that aspect of painting which is 'craft.'

I would formulate the cubist project thus: To realize depth through the extension of volumes and the multiplication of measures aided by a reasoned technique.

This formula was never followed integrally. From the very beginning, the cubist painters singularly reduced its power by losing sight of its first point behind an amalgamation of its second and third points. In effect, under the pretext of gaining a firmer grip on *reality,* they have, for all intents and purposes, multiplied *space* by *time,* naively naming the result *the fourth dimension,* and so creating a heresy wherein they never attain anything except *the reality of the object,* and not *reality itself.* In other words, they studied *progression through space,* which is to say the *material (of the object)* and not *progression through depth,* the *principal (of reality).*[7]

Reduced to the *reality of the object,* of synthetics, cubist investigations became analytical. We saw how quickly the cubists restricted themselves to painting still lifes, and how, confusing effect with cause, they began to include in their compositions authentic materials such as fragments of broken bottles, detachable collars, bits of paper, wood, wood laminate, fabrics, hair, and even the 'object' itself, as it is sold commercially. They found the opposite of what they had sought. The incongruous object had to be 'arranged' pictorially, and ended up falling into the realm of 'fashion.' That is why cubism, which was going to renew the art of painting, never went beyond the limits of 'taste.' It inaugurated the reign of the simulacre, which is, in art, the supreme heresy. (Here we are approaching sorcery, and I am sure that cubism, examined from an occult point of view, will reveal some frightening and terrible secrets. Certain cubist canvases are suggestive of certain black magical procedures, emanating the same unforeseeable, troubling, and diseased charm: literally, they enthrall. They are magic mirrors, tables of sorcery.)

This is why the young generation, healthy, muscular, and very much alive, has detached itself from cubism. And cubism, not withstanding certain of its aspects and the purity of the methods it employed, does not preoccupy the new generation. The new generation has chosen to value exactly what was missing from the cubist experience: the study of depth. The new generation has the sense of reality. It is horrified by void, by destruction, it does not rationalize its vertigo. It stands up. It lives. It wants to construct. Knows that it can only construct through depth. And color gives equilibrium. Color is a sensual element. The senses are reality. This is why the world is colored. The senses construct. The spirit is here. The colors sing. By neglecting color, the cubist painters neglected the emotive principal which holds that in order to be alive (alive in itself, surreal), every work of art must have within it a sensual element, an element which is irrational, absurd, and lyrical, the vital element which takes the work out of limbo.

In relation to what will become the constructive painting of tomorrow, theoretical cubism is like the Trocadero in relation to the Eiffel Tower: without a future, without a tomorrow, without any possible utility. This comparison applies to the group's theoreticians as well. And if, in spite of them, the cubist experience was not entirely negative, we owe it to the group's three antitheoreticians, to three strongly personal painters who represent the three successive phases of cubism: Picasso, Braque, Fernand Léger.

PARIS, MAY 15, 1919

## 4
## MODERNITIES  *For Olga Picasso*

**Pablo Picasso.** Picasso. I know of no temperament more tormented, no mind more restless, no fingers or brushes more rapid or more subtle. His ardor, his skill, his pride, the acrobatics, the love, the cruelty, the elegance, the line, the arabesque, the perversity, the rare, the occult, the acute taste, all relate him to Gilles de Rais and place his work on the same intellectual level as that of a man of letters. This phenomenon is so rare in painting that it is worth noting. I am not saying that Picasso makes literature (like Gustave Moreau), but I maintain that he has been the first to introduce into his paintings certain 'procedures' which were considered, before him, exclusively literary. Neither study nor copy of reality. Real absorption. Contemplation. Magnetism and intuition. The first liberated painter. He creates. He has the mysterious sense of 'correspondences' and possesses the secret cipher of the world. He evokes, he transposes. He lays bare, enigmatically. He insists. He points his finger. He never blinks, because his eyes are transfigured by faith. He affirms life. He adores. Dazzled. In his work there is no Protestant theory, no preconceived lie, but a perpetual religion, a Catholic sensuality, and the stupefying truth of the heart. For he loves. And everything that comes from his hand is animated, always.

Above all else, he is the painter of the true. Man, animal, plant, skeletal abstraction, misunderstood matter, all live, grow, suffer, couple, multiply, disappear, shift, grow again, threaten, become imperative, crystallize. He is the only man in the world who knows how to paint heat, cold, hunger, thirst, perfume, odor, fatigue, lust, envy, paralysis, palpitation, indecision, the obscure tremors of the 'enormous and delicate' subconscious. Then his literary demon intervenes. The painter cuts, pierces, saws, stabs, rips, slashes, strangles. All at once matter is present. At the eye. Enlarged by a notch. This provides us with the key to Picasso's cubism, which is not of a purely aesthetic nature, as his imitators believed it to be, but is rather an exorcism, of a religious nature, which releases the latent spiritual reality of the world. And this again is love. An idealistic transposition.

Given Picasso's particularly literary temperament, his investigations into the material world are, I find, like rapid, pointed, picturesque, arresting notations of depth, 'Natural Histories' à la Jules

Renard. And if Jules Renard has been named the 'eye,' I will call Picasso the 'gaze' – a mystical, tender, sustained, cruel, savage, voluptuous, sadistic gaze.

Since the war, Picasso the master has magnificently isolated himself; he has grown still greater, and has gone still further in his own direction, full of logic, suppleness, and grace. Like his Harlequins, his painting always covers its face with a mask. As for those who have let themselves be taken in by this mystery, too bad! Picasso wants no more disciples. He knows. He is jealous of the face, of the serenity of his painting.

PARIS, MAY 29, 1919

## 5
**MODERNITIES**  *For Madame Braque*

**Braque.** Monsieur Georges Braque is a pure man. He has only one thing in mind: quality. M. Georges Braque is the painter of cubist quality. He is the artist who reviewed all the cubist theories and who chastised each of them for their excesses. He has questioned, interrogated, received confession. Each cubist painter has been led in turn to this austere man's school and has been severely lectured by him. By dint of his authority and his insistence, he has succeeded in subduing these hotheaded painters. He has arrested their growth, breaking off any tendentious branches and pruning the youngest shoots, which he called parasites. This puritan is a hard man who has ended up imposing his own laws, who has kept the entire group in his iron grip. What, then, is his discipline? The doctrine of quality.

Thus, M. Georges Braque is closer to Versailles than to Paris, and as his 'quality' becomes more and more synonymous with virtue, M. Georges Braque appears to be still more directly related to the mentality of Port-Royal. Thanks to him, the cubist painters can be situated fully within the venerable French traditions of cold reason, unswervable stubbornness, and ceremonial pomp. (A Jansenism of which Picasso could be called the feverish and often plaintive Pascal and M. Braque the rigid and didactic logician, the Arnauld, the Grand Arnauld.) Useless to push this analogy further. M. Georges Braque's art is the painting of quality, but before it is pure painting, it is the manifestation of M. Braque's quality. Which he is able to demonstrate by single-handedly recapitulating all the cubist painters' investigations.

M. Braque is, then, a painter of quality. He is dry and precise in his distinguished activity, with suddenly a slight thickening which is a sort of tribute to the thing he has undertaken: the defense of his painting, the patent proof of his quality. (It is also a tiny outlet of the emotion that stirs this painter, and that is so voluntarily repressed.) Every one of M. Braque's canvases is at once a discourse, a panegyric, and an oration.

PARIS, JUNE 19, 1919

## 6

**MODERNITIES**  *For Jeanne Léger*

**Fernand Léger.** Fernand Léger has never been entirely a cubist, in the sense that he has never fallen into the heresy, so dear to the group, of the identity of the object and its representation. There is nothing in him of the recondite, closed, hermetic theoretician. Open to every novelty, he submitted himself to the cubist discipline, as a painter who is deeply concerned with the resources and means of his craft, and he had the rare merit of never losing sight of the first point of the doctrine, the investigation of depth. Even before the war, his canvases already had a look that set them apart from the general run of cubist canvases. They were direct, often brutal, without ever even attempting to be pretty, composed, finished, and they always stayed well within the realm of visual representation. They were more like laboratory experiments than definitive paintings. In them, Léger was studying the cube, and with the literal mind so natural and often so indispensable to painters, he was constructing with inevitable order, studying *successively* volumes, then measures. While even Picasso and Braque were influenced, or troubled, by the virtuosity

of the theoreticians of the fourth dimension, Léger patiently continued to work, going so far in the study of volumes and measures
that he gave birth to Larionov's Russian rayism, and, in addition,
directly influenced the best of the Italian futurist painters. Although
still confused and often incomprehensible, these canvases were the
first works of a new world aesthetic which proclaimed the total
transformation of cubism, and even its disappearance. Léger ad-
vanced into depth and the further he went the closer he got to the
subject.

Then came the war. And at the front, Léger had a revelation of
the depth of today's world.

A shell crater lanced by the world's heavy gaze. All around, foreign countries, the country in the rear and the one in front. Barbed
wire connects these divided countries, links the continents to the
islands, and the Africa of Togoland is very close. Huge swaths of
uniformed men. The picturesque seething of squadrons. The inge-
nious *poilu*. Then new and newer armies of workers. Mountains
of pure primary matter, manufactured products. Parks of engines,
instruments, tools. The painter's mind watches all this intently.
Around him new forms are emerging every day. Enormous volumes
move with agility, thanks to a series of small measures in low gear.
His eye goes from the tin can to the zeppelin, from the caterpillar to
the little spring in a cigarette lighter. An optical signal. A notice. A
poster. The squads of airplanes, the convoys of trucks, gun barrels
shaped like panpipes, American motors, Malaysian daggers, English
jams, international soldiers, German chemicals, the cylinder head
of the 75, everything bears the mark of a formidable unity. Everything is contrast. Ships become invisible on the high seas because
they are overloaded with colors. The picturesque detail enters into
a grandiose ensemble which absorbs even the most jarring antino-
mies. All this for the greater pleasure of the eyes. The heart in the
chest. And the joy of feeling oneself live and die. This is the subject:
human activity and creation. There is nothing anecdotal about it;
no detail can be singled out without evoking the whole.

Today, Léger is master of his subject, and whether he paints the street or the factory he will never forget the complex Unity born of the war, the Power of today, the Spirit and the Letter of Depth.

PARIS, JULY 3, 1919

# 7
## MODERNITIES

**Delaunay.** If *Fernand Léger* is the painter who has gone furthest in the investigation of depth, it must be stated that other cubist painters have gone quite far in that same direction. They will discover, in turn, the human subject who will liberate them from the overly rigid formulas of the school. Among them, I will name the Norwegian *Hellenson,* who paints the still barbaric forms of today: an airplane's insignia, a map, the fragment of a wing, a motor part. His canvases are shaken by blasts of garish colors. A mind which has reached its boiling point is at work and will soon put itself in order and construct. The Mexican *Angel Zarraga,* who had already discovered the subject in 1915, when he painted *Man with Accordion,* in which he found the means of applying liberated cubist formulas. *Hayden,* who continues to paint still lifes in accordance with the school's most rigid formulas, but with such an intensity that he is able to render the molecular life of matter. He is the painter of *interferences.* His excesses have brought him close to the great subject of universal animation. *Léopold Survage,* who has cinematographically grasped the depth of color, but whose canvases are still imbued with unanimist literature. *Forster,* the American, who was killed during the war; he painted only the sun, and the single canvas by him to be exhibited at the Salon of the Independents of 1914 remains one of the best examples of what tomorrow's painting will be. *Marc Chagall,* whose least ambitious watercolor far surpasses the greatest cubist compositions.

But I cannot speak of these painters and their intense lyricism, universal and highly colored, which Guillaume Apollinaire beautifully named 'Orphism,' without speaking of *Robert Delaunay,* the painter of the Eiffel Tower, the inventor of the *simultaneous*. At the end of July 1914, Delaunay abandoned theoretical painting to take on the great human subject in a canvas titled *Caillaux Drama*. At that time, I wrote the following lines on Delaunay's intentions:

*Simultaneous Contrast*

Our eyes reach out to the sun.

A color is not color itself. It is only color in contrast with one or several other colors. A blue is only blue in contrast with a red, a green, an orange, a gray, and all the other colors.

Contrast is not black against white, an opposition, a dissimilarity. Contrast is a similarity. We travel so that we can collect, recollect men, things, and animals. To live with them. We come near them, we do not go away from them. Men differ most in what they have most in common. The two sexes contrast. Contrast is love. Contrast propels stars and hearts. Contrast creates their depth. Contrast is depth. Form.

Today's art is the art of depth.[8]

The word 'simultaneous' is a term of professional jargon, like 're-inforced concrete' in construction, or 'sublimation' in medicine. Delaunay uses it when he works with tower, port, house, man, woman, toy, eye, window, book, when he is in Paris, New York, Moscow, in bed or in the sky. The 'simultaneous' is a technique. The technique shapes primary matter, universal matter, the world.

Poetry is mind into matter.

Sounds, colors, voices, dances, passions, mineral, vegetable, animal, textiles, butchery, chemistry, physics, civilization, offspring, father, mother, paintings, dresses, posters, books, poems, this lamp, this whistle, are the technique, the craft. Simultaneous contrast is the newest improvement in this craft, this technique. Simultaneous contrast is depth perceived. Reality. Form. Construction. Representation.

Depth is the new inspiration. All we see is seen in depth. We live in depth. We travel in depth. I am there. The senses are there. And the spirit.

PARIS, JULY 24, 1919

**On the Parturition of Colors.** M. Léopold Survage is the author of a
theory on the rhythmics of color. He has discovered the genesis of
animated color. His reflections and his studies on contrasting waves
have led him to imagine a film which would show this genesis cine-
matically. Unfortunately, color cinematography is not yet possible. I
will now try to render, in words as *photogenic* as possible, the daring
way in which M. Léopold Survage is able to recreate and decompose
the circular movement of color. He has more than two hundred
pieces of cardboard. You think that you are present at the very creation of the world.

Some red is invading the black screen little by little and soon fills
the entire visual disk. It is a dark, rugged red, wrinkled like kelp. It is
composed of a number of small slats placed side by side. Each of
these slats is tipped by a pustule which quivers slightly and then
bursts like cooling lava. Suddenly the mass of fucus red separates
down the middle. The slats are grouped to the right and to the left;
the activity of the pustules redoubles. A blue stripe appears, rapidly
widens and extends up and down. The frondescent blue branches
out in all directions, and tiny, trembling leaves, quince-shaped like
the leaflets of maidenhair fern grow from it onto the red. The red
slats and the blue leaflets, alternating two by two, gently revolve
now, and then vanish. Only two stringbean-shaped blotches, one
red and the other blue, remain on the screen, facing each other. They
look like two embryos, masculine and feminine. They move toward
each other, connect, break apart, and reproduce by cells and by
clumps of cells. Each spore, each sporocarp, is surrounded by a violet
thread which quickly enlarges, fills out, and swells like a pistil. This
pistil becomes fleshy, its head grows visibly. Little orange lozenges
marble its surface. The lozenges, in turn, grow larger and multiply
with extreme rapidity. The orange and the violet devour each other,
rip each other apart. Branches, limbs, and trunks all tremble, lie
down, rise up. Suddenly the orange blooms like a pumpkin blossom.

The calyx hollows out. At the bottom, two violet pistils lean over a red and blue stamen. Everything turns vertiginously from center to periphery. A ball is forming, of the most dazzling yellow. It looks like a fruit. The yellow explodes. Confetti, multicolored pits, shoot out in all directions. Multiform seeds which fall nobly from high to low. This movement is precipitated and everything falls, dense as hail and uniformly green. Threads are traced, chains, bonds. Twigs, stems, knotted, shooting, or climbing. It looks like a field of grass which tans, grows gray little by little, and slowly melts into a haze of vague forms. Evanescence fading into white. The white steadies and hardens. It freezes.[9] And all around, the void hollows out. The disk, the black disk, reappears and obstructs the visual field.

PARIS, JULY 17, 1919

## 9
## MARC CHAGALL

The Man is alone – very much alone. At the moment of his birth he fell into a washtub.

It's raining, tonight. It's dark. In the silence I hear something like heavy steps in the puddles of water. They are the steps of the cloud-formed mammoth who is moving through the sky. But is there still a sky? Everywhere I touch the Man's smashed heart, his dark heart, smashed, crushed by the heavy steps of pain, and weeping.[10]

It weeps blood.

The wheels of madness spin in the ruts of the sky and splatter God's face with mud. Clouds leap in stupefaction.

The moon looms up suddenly. No, it's the face of God. A desolate, hairless face. A bald head, completely round. The mouth looks as if it's about to burst. Two tears cannot fall from the cheeks.

Listen, I think it's my own head swinging back and forth, desolate, in space.

A cloud moves.

Two bear's feet settle on my shoulders and, up above, a fleshy tongue licks God's eyes. I see only my face in the skies and a dog's tongue hanging out from a cloud, hot . . .

Something moves. A piece of night collapses. Is that you, Woman?

Have pity.

PARIS, APRIL 1912

## 10
### THE EIFFEL TOWER   *For Madame Sonia Delaunay*

. . . In the years 1910 and 1911, Robert Delaunay and I were perhaps the only people in Paris who were talking about machines and art and who were vaguely conscious of the great transformation of the modern world.

At that time I was working with B – – in Chartres, perfecting his airplane, which was to have variable angles of incidence, and Robert, who had worked for a while as a mechanic in a wrought-iron works, was roaming around the Eiffel Tower in his dungarees.

One day, on the way back from Chartres, I fell out of the car at the gate of the Parc Saint-Cloud and broke my leg. I was taken to the nearest hotel, the Hôtel du Palais, kept by Alexandre Dumas père and his son. I stayed there, in that hotel bed, for twenty-eight days, lying on my back with a weight pulling on my leg. I had the bed pushed against the window. So, every morning, when the servant brought me my breakfast and pushed back the shutters and opened the window wide I felt that he was bringing all of Paris to me on his tray. I could see the Eiffel Tower from my window, like a carafe of clear water, the domes of the Invalides and the Pantheon like a teapot and a sugar bowl, and Sacré Coeur, pink and white like a candy box. Delaunay came almost every day to keep me company. He was haunted by the Tower, and the view we had from my window held a great attraction for him. Often he sketched or brought his box of colors.

This is how I was able to witness an unforgettable drama: an artist's struggle with a subject so new that he did not know how to

*Painters* 105

come to grips with it, to subdue it. I have never seen a man struggle and defend himself as much, except perhaps the mortally wounded who were abandoned on the battlefields and who, after two or three days of superhuman effort, fell silent and yielded to the night. But Delaunay remained triumphant.

At this time, Delaunay, who had learned painting from the impressionists, had just finished a more or less brief period among the fauvists. He had just exhibited a series of extremely detailed landscapes and a dozen highly colored portraits. He had met the first cubists at the Salon of the Independents, and all the youthful painters, confronting the loose construction of the impressionist canvases, the confetti of the pointillists, the disjointedness of divisionism, and the hysteria of the fauvists (their own youthful canvases), were increasingly feeling the need to return to more solid forms and to go back, not to one or another art form of the past, which all seemed equally insufficient to them, but to go back to the very sources of plastic form, to put everything back into question, to revise all aesthetic values, to mistrust inspiration, to suppress the subject, to review every technical problem, from the material production of the colors to the use of light sources and the weaving of the canvas. During the six or seven years from 1907 or 1908 to 1914, in the ateliers of young Parisian painters, whole fortunes of patience, analysis, investigation, and erudition were spent, and never did there blaze such an inferno of intelligence! Everything was scrutinized by these painters, contemporary art, the styles of all eras, the plastic expression of all peoples, the theories of all times. Never have so many young painters been seen going into museums to examine in minute detail, study, and confront the technique of the old masters. They sought out the productions of savages and of primitive peoples and the aesthetic vestiges of prehistoric man. They were equally preoccupied with the latest scientific theories of electrochemistry, biology, experimental psychology, and applied physics. Two men, who were not painters, had an enormous influence on the first group of cubist painters: the mathematician Princet, to whom were presented the newest plastic productions and who immediately applied a ciphered formula to them, and the erudite Hellenist Chaudois, who inspected all the theories that made use of citations from Aristotle, Anaximander, and the pre-Socratic philosophers. Maurice Raynal dubbed this frenzied creative and critical activity 'the Investigation of the Fourth Dimension.'

Delaunay, amidst all this, was a simple man, extremely congenial, tall, strong, well equipped for life, a vivid personality, a sensualist. All the brilliant aphorisms, all the superb theories, made his head spin. He reacted in accordance with his temperament, and since he was a born painter, he reacted through color, and Apollinaire sensed this so strongly that in his famous *Aesthetic Meditations,* the book he consecrated to the cubist painters in 1913, he does not speak of Delaunay, unable to situate him amid the other works and theories, but waits to find disciples for him, planning to speak of him in a second volume, for which he found the charming title *The Orphic Painters;* unfortunately, war and death came and took him by surprise.

Here is how Delaunay would work.

He shut himself up in a dark room and nailed the shutters closed. Having prepared his canvas and mixed his colors, he drilled a tiny hole in the shutter. A ray of sunlight filtered into the dark room and he began to paint it, to study it, to take it apart, to analyze its elements of form and color. Without knowing it he was devoting himself to spectral analysis. He worked like this for months, studying pure solar light, discovering sources of emotion outside of any subject. Then he enlarged the hole in the shutter a bit and began to paint the play of colors on a transparent and fragile material like the windowpane. Sparkles, flashes; his little canvases took on the look of synthetic gems, and Delaunay added precious stones, especially pulverized lapis lazuli, to the colors he mixed.[11] Soon the hole in the shutter became so large that Delaunay opened the shutters entirely and flooded the room with daylight. The canvases of this period, which already have a larger format, represent closed windows where the light plays on the glass and on the white chiffon curtains. Finally, he pulled back the curtains and opened the window, and we see a gaping, luminous hole and the roof of the house across the street, lit from behind, hard and solid, a primary, hefty, angular, inclined form.

Delaunay is more and more attracted by what is happening there, outside, and he rediscovers the minuscule play that he studied in a ray of light enlarged to gigantic, enormous dimensions in the luminous ocean that washes down over Paris. The problems are the same, but differently proportioned, on an immense scale.

This is when he paints *The City* and *The Three Graces over Paris*, canvases five or six meters in length, where he tries to bring his academicism into accord with all the novel subjects that he has just discovered: the Seine, with the spire of Notre-Dame, the Parisian suburbs and Alfortville.[12] He finally finds a new subject that permits him to make use of all his discoveries and processes: the Great City. A multitude of new problems are posed, correspondences and contrasts, both spiritual and physical, questions of perspective, of matter, abstract questions of unanimism and synthesis.[13] And the whole personality of Paris pervades him.

More and more, as he spends months contemplating Paris from the top of its highest buildings, more and more his eyes turn toward the Eiffel Tower, its extraordinary form.

This is the moment when I meet him.

I tell him about New York, Berlin, Moscow, prodigious centers of industrial activity scattered over the whole surface of the earth, I tell him about the new way of life that is taking shape, about universal lyricism, and he, hardly more than a boy, who has never left Paris and who has been concerned only with questions of form and color, had guessed all of it as he contemplated the Tower, as he deciphered the first colored posters that were beginning to cover the buildings, as he watched the birth of a mechanical life in the streets.

And now, think of my hotel window, opening onto Paris. This was the very subject of all his preoccupations, a ready-made painting which had to be interpreted, constructed, painted, realized, expressed. And that was very difficult. During that year, 1911, Delaunay painted, I believe, fifty-one canvases of the Eiffel Tower, before achieving any result.

As soon as I could go out, I went with Delaunay to see the Tower. And we traveled around and in the Eiffel Tower.

No known artistic formula could claim to resolve the question of the formal representation of the Eiffel Tower. Realism diminished its height; the ancient Italian laws of perspective narrowed it. The Tower rose above Paris, slender as a hat pin. When we walked away from it, it dominated Paris, rigid and perpendicular; when we walked toward it, it tilted and leaned over us. Seen from the first platform it spiraled, and seen from the top it sank into itself, its legs spread, its neck pulled in. Delaunay wanted to portray Paris around it as well, to situate it. We tried every point of view, we looked at it from all its angles, under all its guises, and its sharpest profile is the one you see from the top of the Passy footbridge. And these thousands of tons of iron, these thirty-five million bolts, this three-hundred-meter tangle of girders, these four arcs spanning one hundred meters, this whole vertiginous mass, played the coquette with us. On certain spring days, it was supple and laughing and opened its parasol of clouds in our faces. In bad weather, it pouted at us, harsh and ungracious, it looked like it was suffering from the cold. At midnight we ceased to exist, all its lights were for New York with which it was already flirting even then; and at noon it told the ships on the high seas what time it was. It was the Tower that taught me Morse code, which allows me today to understand the flickers of radios. And as we roamed around it, we discovered that it exercised a powerful attraction on a lot of people. Lovers climbed to a hundred or two hundred feet above Paris in order to be alone; honeymoon couples came from the provinces or from other countries to visit it; one day we met a boy of fifteen who had come on foot from Dusseldorf to Paris to see it. The first airplanes circled it and saluted it, Santos-Dumont had already chosen it as the goal of his memorable flight in a dirigible, and the Germans had been forced to choose it as their objective during the war, a symbolic objective rather than a strategic one, and I assure you that they could not have taken it: the Parisians would have died for it, and Gallieni had decided to blow it up, our Tower!

So many points of view for examining the case of the Eiffel Tower. But Delaunay wanted to interpret it formally. Finally he succeeded, in the famous painting everyone knows. He contorted the tower to make it fit into his frame, he truncated it and tilted it in order to give it its vertiginous three hundred meters, he employed ten points of view, fifteen perspectives, one section is seen from below, another from above, the houses that surround it are seen from the left, from the right, as the crow flies, from across the street . . .

One day I decided to pay a visit to Monsieur Eiffel himself. It was, moreover, a birthday: twenty-five years for the Tower and seventy-five for Monsieur Eiffel. I was ushered into a small house in Auteuil that was encumbered with a jumble of works of art of all kinds, all of them horribly ugly and useless. The walls of this famous engineer's office were lined with photographs of his greatest creations – bridges, railways, train stations. And as I spoke of my admiration for all this immense effort and for the aesthetic which emerges from his works, and as I praised him above all for the Tower, I saw the old man's eyes open wide, and I had the distinct impression that he thought I was making fun of him! Eiffel himself was a victim of Viollet-le-Duc and almost apologized for having marred Paris with the Tower. Since then, this sort of misunderstanding has ceased to surprise me, but I will note, nonetheless, that the number of engineers who are able to make a contribution to the modern aesthetic grows larger and larger.

– Excerpt from a lecture given on
June 12, 1924, in São Paulo, Brazil

## 11
## Farewell to Painters

I have reprinted here, under the title 'Modernities,' several articles on painting which appeared in the magazine *La Rose Rouge* from May to August 1919.

Alas! I am still waiting for the change, the renewal I predicted. I am becoming more and more convinced that the future of the new generation of French painting has been seriously compromised by amateurs and collectors. We still don't have even our Constantin Guys, the artist who will sketch the elegances, the manners, and the civil war of our time.

The modern painters have profoundly disappointed me, and in bidding them farewell, as a final token of friendship, I give them the following beautiful passage from Kipling. But is there, among all the painters in the salons, the coteries, the schools, the homes of collectors and art dealers,[14] one single man capable of keeping his feet away from the rue la Boétie, and turning them toward a boat or an airplane?

B.C.   PARIS, NOVEMBER 1926

## "Half a Dozen Pictures"

Some men, when they grow rich, store pictures in a gallery. Living, their friends envy them, and after death the genuineness of the collection is disputed under the dispersing hammer.

A better way is to spread your pictures over all earth; visiting them as Fate allows. . . . and the possession of such a gallery breeds a very fine contempt for painted shows and the smeary things that are called pictures.

In the North Pacific, to the right hand as you go westward, hangs a small study of no particular value as compared with some others. The mist is down on an oily stretch of washed-out sea; through the mist the bats-wings of a sealing schooner are just indicated. In the foreground, all but leaping out of the frame, an open rowboat, painted the rawest blue and white, rides up over the shoulder of a swell. A man in blood-red jersey and long boots, all shining with moisture, stands at the bows holding up the carcase of a silver-bellied sea-otter from whose pelt the wet drips in moonstones. Now the artist who could paint the silver wash of the mist, the wriggling treacly reflection of the boat, and the raw red wrists of the man would be something of a workman.

But my gallery is in no danger of being copied at present. Three years since, I met an artist in the stony bed of a brook, between a line of 300 graven, lichened godlings and a flaming bank of azaleas, swearing horribly. He had been trying to paint one of my pictures— nothing more than a big water-worn rock tufted with flowers and a snow-capped hill for background. Most naturally he failed, because there happened to be absolutely no perspective in the thing, and he was pulling the lines about to make some for home consumption. . . .

Luckily, those who painted my gallery were born before man. Therefore, my pictures, instead of being boxed up by lumbering bars of gold, are disposed generously between latitudes, equinoxes, monsoons, and the like, and, making all allowance for an owner's partiality, they are really not so bad.

'Down in the South where the ships never go' – between the heel of New Zealand and the South Pole, there is a sea-piece showing a steamer trying to come round in the trough of a big beam sea. The wet light of the day's end comes more from the water than the sky, and the waves are colourless through the haze of the rain, all but two or three blind sea-horses swinging out of the mist on the ship's dripping weather side. A lamp is lighted in the wheel-house; so one patch of yellow light falls on the green-painted pistons of the steering gear as they snatch up the rudder-chains. A big sea has got home. Her stern flies up in the lather of a freed screw, and her deck from poop to the break of the foc's'le goes under in gray-green water level as a millrace except where it spouts up above the donkey-engine and the stored derrick-booms. Forward there is nothing but this glare; aft, the interrupted wake drives far to leeward, a cut kite-string dropped across the seas. The sole thing that has any rest in the turmoil is the jewelled, unwinking eye of an albatross, who is beating across wind leisurely and unconcerned, almost within hand's touch. It is the monstrous egotism of that eye that makes the picture. By all the rules of art there should be a lighthouse or a harbour pier in the background to show that everything will end happily. But there is not, and the red eye does not care whether the thing beneath its still wings stays or staves.

The sister-panel hangs in the Indian Ocean and tells a story, but is none the worse for that. Here you have hot tropical sunlight and a foreshore clothed in stately palms running out into a still and steamy sea burnished steel blue. Along the foreshore, questing as a wounded beast quests for lair, hurries a loaded steamer never built for speed. Consequently, she tears and threshes the water to pieces, and piles it under her nose and cannot put it under her cleanly. Coir-coloured cargo bales are stacked round both masts, and her decks are crammed and double-crammed with dark-skinned passengers – from the foc'sle where they interfere with the crew to the stern where they hamper the wheel.

The funnel is painted blue on yellow, giving her a holiday air, a little out of keeping with the yellow and black cholera flag at her main. She dare not stop; she must not communicate with any one. There are leprous streaks of lime-wash trickling down her plates for a sign of this. So she threshes on down the glorious coast, she and her swarming passengers, with the sickness that destroyeth in the noonday eating out her heart.

Yet another, the pick of all the East rooms, before we have done with blue water. Most of the nations of the earth are at issue under a stretch of white awning above a crowded deck. The cause of the dispute, a deep copper bowl full of rice and fried onions, is upset in the foreground. Malays, Lascars, Hindus, Chinese, Japanese, Burmans – the whole gamut of race-tints, from saffron to tar-black – are twisting and writhing round it, while their vermilion, cobalt, amber, and emerald turbans and head-cloths are lying under foot. Pressed against the yellow ochre of the iron bulwarks to left and right are frightened women and children in turquoise and isabella-coloured clothes. They are half protected by mounds of upset bedding, straw mats, red lacquer boxes, and plaited bamboo trunks, mixed up with tin plates, brass and copper *hukas*, silver opium pipes, Chinese playing cards, and properties enough to drive half-a-dozen artists wild. In the centre of the crowd of furious half-naked men, the fat bare back of a Burman, tattooed from collar-bone to waist-cloth with writhing patterns of red and blue devils, holds the eye first. It is a wicked back. Beyond it is the flicker of a Malay *kris*. A blue, red, and yellow macaw chained to a stanchion spreads his wings against the sun in an ecstasy of terror. Half-a-dozen red-gold pines and bananas have been knocked down from their ripening-places, and are lying between the feet of the fighters. One pine has rolled against the long brown fur of a muzzled bear. His owner, a bushy-bearded Hindu, kneels over the animal, his body-cloth thrown clear of a hard brown arm, his fingers ready to loose the muzzle-strap. The ship's cook, in blood-stained white, watches from the butcher's shop, and a black Zanzibari stoker grins through the bars of the engine-room-hatch, one ray of sun shining straight into his pink mouth. The officer of the watch, a red-whiskered man, is kneeling down on the bridge to peer through the railings, and is shifting a long, thin black revolver from his left hand to his right. The faithful sunlight that puts everything into place, gives his whiskers and the hair on the back of his tanned wrist just the colour of the copper pot, the bear's fur and the trampled pines. For the rest, there is the blue sea beyond the awnings. . . . Now, disregarding these things and others – wonders and miracles all – men are content to sit in studios and, by light that is not light, to fake subjects from pots and pans and rags and bricks that are called 'pieces of colour.' Their collection of rubbish costs in the end quite as much as a ticket, a first-class one, to new worlds where the 'props' are given away with the sunshine. To do anything because it is, or may not be, new on the market is wickedness that carries its own punishment; but surely there must be things in this world paintable other and beyond those that lie between the North Cape, say, and Algiers. For the sake of the pictures, putting aside the dear delight of the gamble, it might be worth while to venture out a little beyond the regular circle of subjects and – see what happens. If a man can draw one thing, it has been said, he can draw anything. At the most he can but fail, and there are several matters in the world worse than failure. Betting on a certainty, for instance, or playing with nicked cards is immoral, and secures expulsion from clubs. Keeping deliberately to one set line of work because you know you can do it and are certain to get money by so doing is, on the other hand, counted a virtue, and secures admission to clubs. There must be a middle way somewhere, as there must be somewhere an unmarried man with no position, reputation, or other vanity to lose, who most keenly wants to find out what his palette is set for in this life. He will pack his steamer-trunk and get into the open to wrestle with effects that he can never reproduce. All the same his will be a superb failure.[15]

RUDYARD KIPLING

from *Letters of Travel, 1892–1913*

## A Note on This Edition

The texts presented in this volume are all translated from the versions published in the Denoël edition of Cendrars's *Oeuvres complètes* (Paris: 1960–65). (Volume 2 of the Denoël edition contains *L'Eubage* and *La fin du monde filmée par l'Ange Notre-Dame;* volume 4 contains all the other texts that were included in *Aujourd'hui.*)

The notes to the translations frequently indicate changes made by Cendrars on his original manuscripts, as well as on galley proofs or even on his own copies of previous editions. They point to specific areas of concern, all linked to a sense of modernity and Cendrars's search for the most evocative term. As far as I can tell from the available documents, the texts published in the *Oeuvres complètes* after Cendrars's death contain the last revisions he made. As noted in the Bibliography, English translations of *J'ai tué* ('I Have Killed'), *Profond Aujourd'hui* ('Profound Today') and *L'Eubage* ('At the Antipodes of Unity') were published in 1919 and 1922 in *The Plowshare* and *Broom.* Although these first translations are now very rare items, I have been able to consult copies of them. Their style is too outdated to reprint them here. It is, however, significant that literary journals in the United States recognized Cendrars's importance early enough to publish two works by him only a year after their appearance in rare avant-garde editions in France. In the case of *L'Eubage,* the English translation ('At the Antipodes of Unity') was published four years before the original French edition of the work.

## Notes

*Profound Today*

The decision to translate Cendrars's title literally is a deliberate, long-debated one. Unfortunately, the formula is not as effective, poetic, or creative in English as in French. The English 'today' takes on a prosaic matter-of-fact concreteness that loses the abstract ontological value of *aujourd'hui* used as a substantive instead of a temporal adverb. Yet every other possible option loses the multidetermination and simultaneity of meaning contained in the association of the spatial and spiritual connotations of the adjective 'profound' with the temporal immanence of 'today.' This is the paradigmatic formula by which Cendrars characterizes his time in all its facets: intellectual, aesthetic, philosophical, and even factual. The notion of depth in relation to simultaneism, developed later in 'Modernities,' gives further support to this interpretation. Moreover, the original manuscript of *Profond Aujourd'hui* ended with the two words of the title, in a kind of invocation, sealing the form with its meaning. The importance of this concept of depth in relation to the immanence of the present has been discussed in my essay 'Ebauche d'une lecture tantrique de *Profond Aujourd'hui*,' in *Blaise Cendrars: Les Inclassables (1917–1926),* special issue of *La Revue des Lettres Modernes* 782–785 (1986).

1. In *Aujourd'hui,* the collection of these writings published by Grasset in 1931, 'vehicles' replaces 'trams,' and 'motors' replaces 'trolleys.' Cen-

drars's changes indicate his desire to emphasize the technological aspect of modernity.

2. The phrase 'and very real' is omitted in the original manuscript. Cendrars added it by hand on the galley proofs of the 1926 Ecrivains Réunis publication. The addition of this phrase reinforces the theory of simultaneous contrasts; in relation to 'very real,' 'artificial' becomes a new aesthetic category instead of a derogatory qualifier.

3. 'Europe' becomes 'the world' in the 1931 Grasset edition.

4. Cendrars changed 'a' (red one) in manuscript to 'the' (red one) in the 1926 Ecrivains Réunis publication.

5. 'Palamede' in manuscript, the son of the Argonaut of Nauplios whom the Greeks credit with the invention of the game of chess.

6. In manuscript: 'a tram in your chest, a car in your back.' The original version was obviously more evocative of Charlie Chaplin's *Modern Times*.

7. In manuscript: 'scattered' limbs.

8. 'Lives' was added in the original manuscript after 'speaks' and, as mentioned above, the words 'Profound Today' ended the essay after 'You are.'

## I Have Killed

The 1918 edition illustrated by Fernand Léger was extremely well received. Readings were held in literary circles, and people referred to the text as 'the tragic *J'ai tué*.' Renée Riese Hubert has thoroughly analyzed the relationship between Léger's illustrations and Cendrars's text. See Hubert, 'Cendrars and Léger,' *Sud*, 1988.

1. In the first two editions: *un calcul grand de probabilités* (a wealth of probabilities).

2. A typically popular 1914–18 idiom, *petit gris* (literally, 'little gray,' used to refer to tobacco for the soldiers; translated here as 'a pinch of tobacco'), led Cendrars to make up *petit froid* (literally, 'little cold'; translated here as 'a chill down the spine'). The irony of the recurrence of *petit* cannot be rendered in English.

3. *Rimailho:* a type of artillery weapon whose name echoes the archaic French verb *rimailler,* meaning, 'to write bad poetry.'

4. The word *plein* (full) was used in the 1919 Crès edition.

5. *Eustache:* Parisian slang for a kind of switchblade knife invented by a famous underworld figure named Bonnot.

6. The manuscript and galley proofs show that this passage went through three stages before the 1919 Crès edition, which is similar to the Denoël edition from which this translation was made: (*a*) 'cold' is omitted before 'truth'; (*b*) 'cold reason' replaces 'cold truth' (*c*) everything between 'Bonnot's *eustache*' and 'My young athletic past' is omitted.


*In Praise of the Dangerous Life*

In addition to confirming the 1917 composition date (the importance of which is underscored in the introduction to the present volume), the manuscript in the Swiss National Library's Blaise Cendrars Collection in Bern reveals two different angles to this text's theme. A note dated December 5, 1917, sketches an outline according to which the essay would (*a*) examine the theme from the Brahman, or Hindu, point of view (that of the 'wise man of India') in opposition to the American point of view (Teddy Roosevelt's notion of 'the dangerous life'), (*b*) consider the case of the working class, then give the 'American example,' and finally write an apology of work ethics. A second note, dated December 13, contains a revealing reinforcement of the Brahman perspective on action's relationship to 'raw matter' in opposition to Roosevelt's concept of 'dangerous life,' which is denied consideration. What is at stake in this text, therefore, is not the factuality of violent action in 'the dangerous life' but the 'fictuality' of a synchrony between the inner and outer rhythms of modern man and the modern world. Here Cendrars anticipates such works as *The Tao of Physics* and *Where the Wasteland Ends*. The version he adopted for the text's 1926 publication opts for a striking resolution that is very much in tune with his own time.

Cendrars's reference to a 'Brahman's point of view' is of utmost interest. Despite his repeated insistence on the solely Western sources of his spiritualism, it confirms his awareness of a relationship between Eastern philosophies and contemporary attitudes. It also emphasizes the unity linking *Profond Aujourd'hui* to *L'Eubage;* both works are artistic expressions of the essence of contemporaneity, rather than of its exterior manifestations.

Cendrars's openly esoteric preoccupations clearly distinguish his work from the futurist project.

    1. In the 1926 edition 'authority' replaced 'initiative.'

## The ABCs of Cinema

Documents consulted in Bern prove that, once again, the genesis of this text dates back to the pivotal year 1917. They also reveal that Cendrars's initial project was far more ambitious than the text eventually published in 1921. An outline dated November 1917 projects eight chapters, ranging from a broad introductory overview of the period to a consideration of the future poetics of the cinema. Projected chapters on Schopenhauer and on mysticism and the cinema suggest that Cendrars's intention was to write a wide-ranging reflection on the significance of cinematographic arts in contemporary aesthetics. One of the titles Cendrars initially toyed with, 'Le livre du cinéma' (The book of the cinema), clearly indicates that he was contemplating a far more comprehensive study than the one he finally produced. The manuscript that remains from this initial plan is only a one-page document ending at 'life of the depths.' It was first published in *La Rose Rouge* 7 (June 12, 1919): 108, and in *Promenoir,* March 1921.

    1. A complete study of this text will be the object of a forthcoming publication of the University of Bern's Centre d'Etudes Blaise Cendrars (CEBC). Hence I note here only the major additions and omissions that indicate the various directions Cendrars considered taking. The 1917 manuscript inserts here: 'There are eleven movements in space.'

    2. Insert in 1917 manuscript: 'After the poets, the musicians, and the architects, the scientists erect pyramids.'

    3. Insert in 1917 manuscript: 'Today that machine creates man.'

    4. In the 1919 *Rose Rouge* article, 'luminous' replaces 'fatal,' and 'mathematical' replaces 'astronomical.'

    5. In English in the original.

    6. Italicized words appear in English in the original.

    7. In addition to the 1917 handwritten fragment, two typed copies of the manuscript are known to exist. One, signed 'Rome, April 21, 1921,'

omits the ABC-Z parts. The other contains everything but the italicized subtitles. These variations are indicative of Cendrars's concern for the 'splicing' of a text in relation to the reader.

### The End of the World Filmed by the Angel of Notre Dame

1. William Booth, a British reformer born in Nottingham (1829–1912), was the founder of the Salvation Army. 'Rudolf Schreiner' is probably a (deliberate?) misspelling of Rudolph Steiner (1861–1925), the Austrian philosopher, author of *Theosophy* (1904), *Initiation* (1904), and *The Occult Sciences* (1909). Joseph Péladan (1859–1918) was a French writer, author of a nineteen-volume treatise on Roman decadence. Versed in occult sciences, he was known as a magus in French theosophic circles and gave himself the title of Sar.

2. Nahum: Hebrew prophet of the seventh century B.C. The Book of Nahum prophesies the fall of Nineveh. Amos: one of the twelve 'little' Hebrew prophets (eighth century B.C.). Micah: Hebrew prophet (740–687 B.C.). The Book of Micah is particularly famous for its prophecy that the one who will rule Israel will be born in Bethlehem.

### The Eubage; or, At the Antipodes of Unity

*Eubage:* A Celtic priest dedicated to the observation of nature and astronomy. Commissioned by Jacques Doucet, *L'Eubage* was written in seven installments that were mailed to Doucet on a monthly basis: May 3, 1917, chapters 1 and 2; June 23, 1917, chapters 3 and 4; July 23, 1917, chapter 5; September 1917, chapter 6; November 1917, chapter 7; December 1917, chapter 8; January 2, 1918, chapters 9–12. All the general studies of Cendrars listed in the Bibliography include analyses of *L'Eubage.* A more specific study of its genesis and of Cendrars's correspondence with Jacques Doucet is carried out by Yvette Bozon-Scalzitti in her *Blaise Cendrars; ou, La Passion de l'Ecriture* (Lausanne: L'Age d'Homme, 1977), 295–99.

In *Mystère et splendeur de Jacques Doucet* (Paris: Jean Claude Lattes, 1984), 245–49, François Chapon evokes the adventure of *L'Eubage.* Partially inspired by Camille Flammarion's *L'astronomie populaire* (Paris, 1880), this surreal narrative was initially going to be illustrated with scientific plates. The illustrations by the Polish engraver Jean Hecht (Lodz, Poland, 1891–Paris, 1951) chosen for the 1926 Au Sans Pareil publication cast the text in an entirely different light. Jean Carlo Flückiger will make a detailed study of this first choice of plates in a complete edition of *L'Eubage* forthcoming from the University of Bern's CEBC. He has already given a glimpse of their content in 'A propos de *L'Eubage*,' in *Blaise Cendrars: Les Inclassables (1917–1926),* special issue of *La Revue des Lettres Modernes* 782–785 (1986).

The texts sent by Cendrars to Jacques Doucet were followed by an unpublished appendix on the *perpetuum mobile,* an extremely significant point of interest for the magus of the simultaneous in today's world of fragmentation.

1. Actually 'Achernar,' or 'Achernard,' as established by Flückiger, 'A propos de *L'Eubage*,' 137–38.

2. Flückiger points out the double meaning of the word 'hepatite' (a kind of barite that becomes fetid when rubbed or heated). According to him, Cendrars chose it not only for its gemological value, but also for its double meaning connected to intoxication. Ibid., p.139.

3. 'Hemospasia': a bloodletting technique in which vacuum is employed to draw blood out of the body.

4. Another of Cendrars's major sources for this text was Robert Fludd (1574–1637), a famous British alchemist and the inventor of the weather glass. Fludd wrote the monumental *Utriusque cosmi, majoris silicet et minoris, metaphysica, physica atque technica historia* (A metaphysical, physical, and technical history of the macrocosm and microcosm), among scores of other treatises on chiromancy, astrology, physiognomy, music, and so on. Heir to the hermetic and cabalistic tradition of the Renaissance, he was an adept of Paracelsus and the occult sciences and became attracted to the Rosicrucians during his visit to Germany. Cendrars mentions his book on chiromancy in a 1907 diary.

The 'most thorough treatise on the music of the spheres' to which the Eubage refers actually appears in the first volume of Fludd's treatise *Tractatus primus de metaphysico macrocosmi et creaturarum illius ortu* in a chapter entitled 'De musica mundana.' Jean Carlo Flückiger ('Le pouvoir secret de la musique,' in *Continent Cendrars I* [Neuchâtel: La Baconnière, 1986],

47) explains how Fludd's paradigm of two opposite pyramids (*pyramis formalis* and *pyramis materialis*) that establish a vitalizing flow of energy between their negative and positive poles, as well as his theory of cosmic music, provided Cendrars with a weltanschauung that answered both his spiritual quest and his naturalistic sensuality. There is no doubt that Fludd's Paracelsian tradition would attract the modernist poet in search of unity at the 'antipodes' of unity.

## Painters

Mrs. Errazuris, the well-known sponsor and supporter of several avant-garde artists, particularly Picasso at one point, was a very close friend of Cendrars, who lived at her place in Biarritz on and off for several years.

1. In *La Rose Rouge:* 'for five years' instead of 'since the war.'

2. The phrase 'At the 1919 Independent show,' which appears in the *Rose Rouge* original, was omitted from the version of the text reprinted in the 1931 Grasset volume *Aujourd'hui.* Three other references to the 'Independent show' were removed from this article as well. Cendrars's intent to place his text beyond the topical journalistic concerns of the time is evident.

3. Reference to the 'Independent show' removed in the reprint.

4. Reference to the 'Independent show' removed in the reprint.

5. Reference to the 'Independent show' removed in the reprint.

6. Cendrars's note: 'Léonce Rosenberg's gallery.'

7. Cendrars's note: 'The Futurists, for their part, divided space and time and studied only the *dynamism* (of the object) and never the *rhythmic principle* (of matter), or, in other words, *progression on a chart* and not *progression in space, mechanics* and not *chemistry,* which at least some of the cubists had hit upon.'

8. Unpublished fragments of the manuscript for 'Painters' reveal that Cendrars gave a great deal of thought to the concept of depth. The notion of depth for him is like a sixth sense, a mode of being and a state of mind, 'a new state of consciousness and not a theory of the intellect.' He perceives it as inherently linked to new forms of life.

9. Up to this point, this is the same paragraph that is incorporated, with

infinitely minor changes, into chapter 7 of *The Eubage*. The fact that a text inspired by Survage becomes the core of a climactic moment in a description of an alchemical experiment that resolves all colors into an ultrawhite disk around a primeval whirling spiral underscores Cendrars's esoteric notions of the creative act.

10. A totally different and longer text on Chagall was written by Cendrars on April 7, 1911. I cannot include it here, unfortunately, since it will be presented by the CEBC in one of its forthcoming publications. It is interesting to note, however, that in that text Cendrars addresses himself directly to Chagall, sharing his own feelings with him rather than giving a poetic transposition of the paintings. His praise of Chagall's *Violinist* is straightforward: 'The most beautiful painting at the Independent show this year.'

11. A copy of the 1931 Grasset edition of *Aujourd'hui* contains corrections by Cendrars that were never incorporated in subsequent reprints. Here, *surtout* (especially) is replaced by 'primarily like Fra Angelico.'

12. In his copy of the 1931 Grasset edition, after 'the Seine,' Cendrars added 'which goes up to Charenton.'

13. In that same copy of the Grasset volume, 'Poetic' was added before 'correspondence.'

14. The word 'art' was added by the translator, but Cendrars himself had inserted it by hand on his copy of the 1931 edition.

15. Rudyard Kipling, *Letters of Travel, 1892–1913* (New York: Scribner, 1920), 81–90. Cendrars took the quotation from Kipling, *Lettres de Voyage* (Paris: Payot, 1922). The cuts in the passage were made by Cendrars.

# Bibliography

This bibliography is restricted to publications that concern the texts translated in this volume and works by Cendrars published in English. For a complete bibliography of Cendrars's works and major critical studies on him, consult Jay Bochner's or Monique Chefdor's publications in English, Yvette Bozon-Scalzitti's in French, and Monique Chefdor's chronology in *Europe* 566 (June 1976). The out-of-print Club Français du Livre edition of Cendrars's *Oeuvres complètes,* vol. 15 (Paris, 1971), contains a detailed bibliography of Cendrars's publications, which I have updated here by directly consulting the original publications. Bibliographical information on reprints of Cendrars's works, critical studies, and translations in all languages is regularly updated in the Blaise Cendrars International Society bulletin *Feuille de Routes.*

## I. CURRENT EDITIONS AVAILABLE IN FRENCH

1960–65  *Oeuvres complètes.* 8 vols. Paris: Denoël. Reissued, 1987. Volume 2 contains *La fin du monde filmée par l'Ange Notre-Dame* and *L'Eubage;* volume 4 includes all other texts collected in *Aujourd'hui.*

1987  *Aujourd'hui, suivi de Essais et réflexions.* Paris: Denoël. Contains *Profond Aujourd'hui, J'ai tué, Eloge de la vie dangereuse, L'ABC du cinéma,* and 'Peintres' ('Modernities' 1–8, from the series published in *La Rose Rouge,* together with the three other articles added by Cendrars in the 1931 Grasset edition of *Aujourd'hui*). In addition the volume contains a short section on poets and reprints of excerpts from *Inédits secrets.*

1991    *Oeuvres Completes,* vol. 9. 'J'écris. Ecrivez-moi' Correspondence with Jacques Henry Levesque 1924–1959, edited by Monique Chefdor. Paris: Denoël.

II. PREVIOUS EDITIONS OF WORKS TRANSLATED IN THIS VOLUME

The history of the publication of these avant-garde texts by Cendrars constitutes an informative document on their reception, hence the inclusion of information on translations into other European languages besides English. Previous English translations are listed separately below.

*Profond Aujourd'hui*

1917    Paris: La Belle Edition. Published as a duodecimo booklet with five drawings by Angel Zarraga. 276 copies.

1919    *La Revue Romande* (Lausanne) 3, 10 (October 15): 1–7.

1921    *Cosmopolis* (Madrid) 33 (September): 13–17. Translated by G. de la Torre.

1926    Paris: Les Ecrivains Réunis. Published as a sextodecimo booklet. 576 copies.

*J'ai tué*

1918    Paris: La Belle Edition. With five drawings by Fernand Léger. 176 copies.

1919    Paris: Editions Georges Crès. With a portrait of Cendrars by Fernand Léger.

1920    *D'Aci d'Alla* (Barcelona), May. With seven drawings by E. Ferrer. Translated by Joan Estelrich.

*Eloge de la vie dangereuse*

1926    Paris: Les Ecrivains Réunis. Published as a sextodecimo booklet. 575 copies.

*L'ABC du cinéma*

1919    *Les hommes du jour* (Paris), February 8. Fragment.

1919    *La Rose Rouge* 7 (June 12): 108. Fragment.

1921    *Promenoir* (Lyons) 2 (May): 28–29. Fragment.

1921    *Cosmopolis* (Madrid) 33 (September): 18–19. Fragment. Translated by G. de la Torre.

1926    Paris: Les Ecrivains Réunis. Published as a sextodecimo booklet. 575 copies.

1931    *Der Querschnitt* (Berlin), January 15. Fragment.


*La fin du monde filmée par l'Ange Notre-Dame*

1916    'La fin du monde.' *La Caravane* (Paris), October. (Note how the title changes in 1918 and 1919.)

1918    'Le film de la fin du monde.' *Mercure de France* (Paris), December 1, 419–29.

1919    *La fin du monde filmée par l'Ange Notre-Dame, Roman.* Paris: Editions de la Sirène. With colored illustrations by Fernand Léger.

1949    *La fin du monde filmée par l'Ange Notre-Dame.* With a preface by the author. Paris: Pierre Seghers. Reissued with a cover by Fernand Léger in 1956.

1949    Adaptation for the radio, with music by Darius Milhaud. French Radio Broadcasting System, December 31.


*L'Eubage, aux antipodes de l'unité*

1926    Paris: Au Sans Pareil. With five engravings by Jean Hecht. 1,100 copies.


'Peintres' ('Modernités' and other writings on painters)

1919    'Modernité 1.' *La Rose Rouge* 1 (May 3): 13.

1919    'Modernité 2.' *La Rose Rouge* 2 (May 9): 27.

1919    'Modernité 3.' *La Rose Rouge* 3 (May 15): 33.

1919    'Modernité 4.' *La Rose Rouge* 5 (May 29): 77. Reprinted in *Vogue* (Paris), April 1929, and in *Le Centaure* (Paris) 9 (June 1929).

1919    'Modernité 5.' *La Rose Rouge* 8 (June 19): 113.

1919    'Modernité 6.' *La Rose Rouge* 10 (July 3): 155. Reprinted in *Selection* (Anvers), 1929.

1919    'Modernité 7.' *La Rose Rouge* 13 (July 24): 204. 'Le contraste simul-
        tané.' Reprinted in *Aktion* (Berlin) 11:134.
1919    'Modernité 8.' *La Rose Rouge* 12 (July 17): 181. Reprinted in *Broom*
        3 (October 1922), translated by Harold Loeb; and in *L'Eubage*
        (Paris: Au Sans Pareil, 1926).
1914    'Marc Chagall.' *Les Soirées de Paris* (Paris), June 15.


*Aujourd'hui*

1931    Paris: Editions Bernard Grasset. Published as an octavo book
        with a drawing by Conrad Moricand: 'The unique hand of Blaise
        Cendrars.' 240 pages. The first publication of collected prose
        works by Cendrars, the volume contains all the texts listed above
        plus 'La Tour Eiffel,' an unpublished lecture delivered in São
        Paulo on June 12, 1924, and 'Pour prendre congé des peintres,' an
        excerpt from Rudyard Kipling, *Lettres de Voyage* (Paris: Payot,
        1922).


III. WORKS BY CENDRARS IN ENGLISH TRANSLATION

1919    'I Have Killed' (*J'ai tué*). Translated by Harold Ward. *Plowshare*
        6/7.
1922    'Profound Today' (*Profond Aujourd'hui*). Translated by Harold
        Loeb. *Broom* 1 (January): 265–67.
1922    'The Cabinet of Doctor Caligari.' Review of the film. Translated
        from *Feuilles Libres* 4 (June–July). *Broom* 2 (July): 351.
1922    'At the Antipodes of Unity' (*L'Eubage*). Translated by Matthew
        Josephson. *Broom* 3 (October): 182–93.
1926    'The Days of 49' (abridged version of *L'Or*). Hearst's *International*
        combined with *Cosmopolitan* (October).
1926    *Sutter's Gold* (*L'Or*). Translated by Henry Longan Stuart. New
        York: Harper. Reissued in 1936, 1954. Reprints. London: Heine-
        mann, and New York: Grosset & Dunlap, 1936.
1927    *African Saga* (*Anthologie nègre*). Translated by Margery Bianco.
        New York: Boards, Payson & Clark. Reprint. New York: Negro
        University Press, 1969.

1929     *Little Black Stories for Little White Children* (*Petits Contes nègres pour les enfants des Blancs*). New York: Harcourt, Brace.

1931     *Panama* (*La Prose du Transsibérien*, 'Panama,' excerpts from *Kodak* and from part 1 of *Feuilles de route*). Translated and with an introduction and illustrations by John Dos Passos. New York: Harper. Reprint. With an introduction by George Reavey. *Chelsea Review* 3 (Winter 1959): 3–25.

1931     'John Paul Jones.' In *European Caravan*, edited by Samuel Putnam, 199–204. New York: Brewer, Warren & Putnam.

1931     *I Have No Regrets* (*Feu le lieutenant Bringolf*). Translated by Warren B. Wells. Edited by Blaise Cendrars. London: Jarrolds.

1948     *Antarctic Fugue* (*Le Plan de l'Aiguille*). Translation unsigned. London: Pushkin Press; New York: Anglobooks.

1962     *Selected Writings* (*Pâques à New York, La Prose du Transsibérien*, two poems from *Documentaires*, five from *Feuilles de route*, and selections from prose works). Edited and with an introduction by Walter Albert. Preface by Henry Miller. New York: New Directions. Reissued, 1966.

1966     *To the End of the World* (*Emmène-moi au bout du monde*). Translated by Alan Brown. London: Peter Owen. Reprint. New York: Grove Press, 1968.

1966     'The Art of Fiction' and 'Manolo Secca' (selections from *Blaise Cendrars vous parle* and *L'Homme foudroyé*, respectively), and eleven poems. Translated by Ron Padgett. Introduction by William Brandon. *Paris Review* 10, no. 37: 105–43.

1968     *Moravagine*. Translated by Alan Brown. London: Peter Owen. Reprints. New York: Doubleday, 1970; London: Penguin, 1979.

1968     'Two Portraits: Gustave Le Rouge and Arthur Cravan' (From *L'Homme foudroyé* and *Le Lotissement du ciel*). Translated by William Brandon. *Paris Review* 11, no.42: 157–70.

1968     'Four Poems.' Translated by Tom Clark and Ron Padgett. *Works* 1, no.3:39–42.

1968     'The Transsiberian Express." Translated by Anselm Holls. In *Evergreen Review Reader*, 621–30. New York: Grove Press.

1970     *The Astonished Man* (*L'Homme foudroyé*). Translated by Nina Rootes. London: Peter Owen.

1972    *Planus* (*Bourlinguer*). Translated by Nina Rootes. London: Peter Owen.

1972    'The Prose of the Transsiberian and of Little Jehanne de France' (as printed, with article of the same title, in *Der Sturm* [November 1913]: 184–85). Translated by Roger Kaplan. *Chicago Review* 24, no.3: 3–21.

1973    *Lice* (*La Main coupée*). Translated by Nina Rootes. London: Peter Owen.

1976    *Complete Postcards from the Americas: Poems of Road and Sea* (*Documentaires, Feuilles de route,* 'Sud-Americaines'). Translated and with an introduction by Monique Chefdor. Berkeley: University of California Press.

1979    *Selected Poems.* Translated by Peter Hoida. Introduction by Mary Ann Caws. London: Penguin.

1983    *Shadow* (excerpts from *Petits Contes nègres pour les enfants des Blancs*). Translated and illustrated by Marcia Brown. New York: Scribner.

1984    *Gold* (*L'Or*). Translated by Nina Rootes. New York: Michael Kesand. Reissued, 1989.

1985    *A Night in the Forest (First Fragment of an Autobiography)* (*Une nuit dans la forêt. Premier fragment d'une autobiographie*). Translated by Margaret Kidder Ewing. Columbia: University of Missouri Press.

1987    *Dan Yack* (*Le Plan de l'Aiguille,* with an 'epilogue' from *Les Confessions de Dan Yack*). Translated by Nina Rootes. London: Peter Owen.

## IV. CRITICAL STUDIES

Bochner, Jay. *Blaise Cendrars: Discovery and Recreation.* Toronto: University of Toronto Press, 1978.

Bozon-Scalzitti, Yvette. *Blaise Cendrars; ou, La Passion de l'Ecriture.* Lausanne: L'Age d'Homme, 1977.

Caws, Mary Ann. 'Blaise Cendrars: A Cinema of Poetry.' In *The Inner Theatre of Recent French Poetry.* Princeton: Princeton University Press, 1972.

Caws, Mary Ann. 'From Prose to the Poem of Paris or Cendrars's *Tour.*' In *Dada Surrealism* 9. New York: Wittenborn Art Books, 1979.

Chadourne, Jacqueline. *Blaise Cendrars, poète du cosmos.* Paris: Seghers, 1973.

Chefdor, Monique. Introduction to *Complete Postcards from the Americas,* 1–41. Berkeley: University of California Press, 1976.

Chefdor, Monique. *Blaise Cendrars.* Twayne World Authors Series, 571. Boston: G. K. Hall, 1980.

Chefdor, Monique, and Claude Leroy, eds. Special issue, *Blaise Cendrars: Les Inclassables (1917–1926). Revue des Lettres Modernes* 782–785 (1986). Texts presented by Claude Leroy. Entire issue devoted to the texts translated in this volume; articles by Monique Chefdor, Michel Decaudin, Jean Carlo Flückiger, J. P. Goldenstein, Maurice Mourier, Michèle Touret.

Flückiger, Jean Carlo. 'Le pouvoir de la musique: A propos de *L'Eubage.*' In *Continent Cendrars I,* 42–47. Neuchâtel: La Baconnière, 1986.

Hubert, Renée Riese. 'Cendrars and Léger." *Sud,* 1988, 103–23. Special issue, *Blaise Cendrars,* ed. F. J. Temple, for the Blaise Cendrars Centennial Colloquium, Cérisy La Salle, 1987.

Horrex, Susan. 'Blaise Cendrars and the Aesthetics of Simultaneity.' *Dada Surrealism* 6 (Queens College Press, 1976).

Levin, Gail. 'Blaise Cendrars and Morgan Russel: Chronicle of a Friendship.' *Dada Surrealism* 9 (Wittenborn Art Books, 1979).

Perloff, Marjorie. *The Futurist Moment.* Chicago: University of Chicago Press, 1987. Several pages on *Profound Today* and references to 'Modernities.'

Pilard, Philippe. 'Cendrars: Cinéma de rêve, rêve de cinéma.' In *Sud,* 19ff, 123–33. Special issue, *Blaise Cendrars,* ed. F. J. Temple, for the Blaise Cendrars Centennial Colloquium, Cérisy La Salle, 1987.

Thibault, Jean François. 'Cendrars et Survage, rythmes colorés.' In *Blaise Cendrars, vingt ans après,* 183–89. Ed. Claude Leroy. Paris: Klincksieck, 1983.